Far-Away Places
Lessons in Exile

HOWARD R. WOLF

ARTZY
BOOKS
JERUSALEM ◆ NEW YORK

Far-Away Places
Published by ARTZY Books

Text Copyright © 2007 by Howard R. Wolf

Cover Design: Zippy Thumim
Typesetting: Tiffen Studios
Editor: Ovadya di Israel
Editorial and Production Manager: Daniella Barak

Hard Cover ISBN: 978-1-932687-99-6

E-mail: sales@ARTZYBooks.com

Printed in Israel

*F*or My Father,

Abraham Wolf (1908–1998),

who, born into poverty and unable to travel,

gave me my first atlas and quizzed me about

far-away places.

CREDITS

Far-Away Places
> First published in India: *Dialog: An Interdisciplinary Journal*,
> No. 12, Spring 2004.
> © Howard R. Wolf 2004.

Wagner's Shed: Property and Fantasy
in the American Backyard
> First published in *Hawaii Review*, Fall 1987.
> © Howard R. Wolf 1987.
> Reprinted by *Farmer's Market*, Winter 1988.
> © Howard R. Wolf 1988.

Blueprint for a Changing World:
Some Roles of American Studies Overseas Today
> First published in *Canadian Review of Comparative Literature*,
> March/June 1993. © Howard R. Wolf 1993.

An American in Anatolia
> First published in *Journal of the Association of International
> Education Administrators*, Spring 1986. © Howard R. Wolf 1986.

Last Days of Chua X:
Women, Work, and the Late Colonial Tropics
> First published in *Farmer's Market*, Fall 1990.
> © Howard R. Wolf 1990.

A Passenger to India
> First published in *Farmer's Market*, Fall 1989.
> © Howard R. Wolf 1989.

Farewell to Hong Kong: A Cultural Valedictory
> First published in *Asian Culture* (Taiwan), Fall 1996.
> © Howard R. Wolf 1996.

Homage to Broward County: The End of the Littoral
> First published in *The Diasporic Imagination: Asian-American
> Writing* (Prestige/India), ed. Somdatta Mandal, 2000.
> © Howard R. Wolf 2000.
> Reprinted by *Out of Line*, 2003. © Howard R. Wolf 2003.

The New South Africa: Journey Toward Dignity
> First published in *Textures 15*, Fall 2002.
> © Howard R. Wolf 2002.

Confessions of an Anxious Traveler
> First published in Finnish in *Psykoterapia* (Finland), 2002.
> © Howard R. Wolf 2002.

ACKNOWLEDGMENTS

I wish to thank Lucy G. Carson for the careful preparation of the manuscript. Without her patient help, this book would not have seen the light of day. I would like to thank as well Daniella Barak and Ovadya di Israel for their editorial assistance, without which this book - in its final form - would not have been possible.

TABLE OF CONTENTS

PREFACE

As a young American who became aware of the world during the Second World War, I was an instant patriot and wanted to be sent to some far-flung part of the globe so that I could, like my uncles and summer camp counselors, fight the fascists and save the people who were suffering. I don't think I knew, then, the explicit horrors of the Nazi terror, but some refugees and DPs ("displaced persons") had come to our neighborhood, even our building. For a while, we had Italian neighbors in our apartment house who looked gaunt and frightened. I knew by the age of ten that I wanted to go out into this larger world so that I could, in some way, help, though I didn't know what that would mean.

At a somewhat later age, during my first year of high school, I discovered English and American literature and wanted immediately, without explanation or warrant, to be a writer. I learned quickly that many of these writers had traveled. And it seemed that all the American ones had gone to Paris in the 1920s. The legacy of Hemingway and Fitzgerald acted as a powerful magnet upon the ore of my still-buried creative imagination. I understood that writers traveled in order to write and wrote about their travels in order to make sense of their experience. I could see that there was an inner and outer map and that the two cartographic spheres were related. If one wanted to form an image of a whole world, one had to go abroad.

The actual journeys turned out to be quite different from the imagined ones. The essays in this collection (ca. 1982–2004) chart some of these differences in the order in which they were discovered. All together, they make up something like a cultural autobiography of the world, as I've known it.

In recasting these essays, to some degree, to shape a whole, I have at the end of each chapter added a section – "Re-vision" – in which I revisit some of my assumptions and conclusions in the light and shadow of the past decade or so. These re-visions (codas, as it were) touch upon my personal history and the larger history of the places in which I have lived, taught, and written and in which I observed, absorbed, and recorded the life of my surroundings. And these added sections try to connect the personal and global like overlapping geographical transparencies. The original essays remain largely unchanged, except for the clarification of "Americanisms," but the re-visions explore some of the latent depths and altered significance of these immanent cultural autobiographies.

I look back in these codas at myself living in the *then* present, at myself looking *then* to the future as well as the past. Some of that future is already behind us, and some of that past (a reemergence of "traditionalisms" of various kinds) is now embedded in our present and points to the future, a kind of road map. At the time when the first of these essays was written, America was still looking primarily at the U.S.S.R. as the world power that might set the world ablaze. Then, after the collapse of the Soviet Union in the early 1990s, the rising suns of the South China coasts and the Pacific Rim cast their light across the world, and the many faces of Islam were often the images we saw on CNN.

These changes expanded, but did not negate, the core of my experiences any more than the death of a parent or the

8

birth of a child negates one's memory of childhood or one's relationship with a partner. In fact, we only can understand the meaning of these reversals, losses and gains, in the light of the original experience. Part of what we learn in the present is what we didn't understand in the past about it. This may teach us how better to understand the present.

In the fullness of time, all aspects of time and consciousness and the connection between them undergo some form of revision. It is not without significance that fairy tales begin, "Once upon a time." When the fairy tales are very good, "a" time becomes "all" time. It's my hope and intention that these essays – textured and shaped entries in my chronicle of life lived often outside of America – will stand as artifacts which can bear the weight of their own existential authenticity as well as the impress of some reconstruction (re-vision).

I want to preserve the original mosaics and to put them at the same time in an enlarged historical context – not unlike an explanatory historical note that explains some aspect of an obscure symbol at an ancient site. In saying this, I reflect an important part of my life in the past four years when I have visited Israel six times during which periods I have seen many ancient sites whose layers of archeology and history are not unrelated to what I'm saying here.

I had no clue when I wrote "Homage to Broward County: The End of the Littoral," a personal essay about Florida, that the grandson who is a central figure in it would be living in Israel six years later. He is still the same child in the same photograph that is the centerpiece of the essay, but the role he plays in the Jewish-American story of immigration, assimilation, and, in some cases, expatriation is now enlarged. My daughter's quest for a homeland has taught me a great deal about everyone's search for a place of belonging. Birth is a kind of exile, according to Otto Rank, one of Freud's early disciples, and we spend our lives looking for new terms of wholeness. Plato has something to say about this in the "Symposium." Exodus and return, the Fall and redemption, are universal terms. I hear an old college song as I write this sentence, "Long Ago and Far Away."

In some poignant way, this grandchild, who now speaks Hebrew fluently, is a recreation of my grandfather who barely could speak English and with whom I barely could communicate when we would meet for lunch on Broadway. My daughter and grandson (now grandsons) have reversed the direction of history for me, as I have reversed it temporarily by living outside of America at various points. I record some of these reversals in some of these essays; and revisiting sites of the past to discover the origins of the present is one of the unifying themes of this book.

I now can see more intimations of the future in the past; but to change that past in any important way would be to falsify precisely the specific ways in which the past adumbrated the future. To some extent, traveling to a place which has an association with one's personal, familial, and cultural past is not unlike the process of revision: the past is rediscovered in the present even as one learns how the present is informed by the past. It's a two-way street, and one meets oneself simultaneously walking in two directions. This is as close to relativity theory as I'm likely to get; but, as I often say, everything is relative except one's relatives.

This book can be read in several ways: straight through (with or without "Re-visions"); in free-standing chapters selected in whatever order the reader wishes; and one could read the "Re-visions" before or after these options, depending on one's taste and mood. Needless to say, I would prefer the whole journey from Turkey to Hong Kong and points North and South.

CHAPTER ONE

FAR-AWAY
PLACES

*H*ow and when did I become interested in traveling and writing about far-away places? I suppose I could try to go back to, or invent an origin of, this impulse, beginning with the dawn of consciousness, but I don't want to launch a theoretical project. An old photograph gives me a clue. I am standing somewhere in Fort Tryon Park in Washington Heights, Upper Manhattan, New York City, on a bluff overlooking the Hudson River, the neighborhood of my childhood. I did not realize until years later that I had grown up in the shadow of the American Revolution. The past enlarges and shifts its meaning as we live into the future – not unlike the process of writing about the past.

One can see in the distance the tower and ramparts of the Cloisters (the Medieval Branch of the Metropolitan Museum of Art). And one can see beyond this place the green cliffs of the Palisades on the New Jersey side of the Hudson River – all together, a pretty spectacular site (and sight) for an American boyhood.

I was aware of Fort Tryon Park and the Cloisters in early childhood as a pleasant and fascinating place, though I couldn't have named the source of the fascination. It was a place for sledding in winter, on those rare occasions when there was enough snow for sledding in New York City (the Great Blizzard of 1947) and for walking with one's family in the summer, on those rare occasions when my family walked together. The Fort Tryon Park of the 1940s belongs to a lost era. Before television and other electronic media became the focus of domestic life, families did more things together outdoors.

There were glimpses of pheasants in wooded areas, and there were real Sunday painters, people with oils and easels who themselves might have been subjects of a Seurat or Renoir painting. This was my introduction to Europe before I knew that I wanted to, had to, go to the Continent, as it still was called then, as part of my education. The Cloisters was, literally and symbolically, part of Europe in America. Many of the actual structural and architectural elements of the several cloisters – Saint Guilhem, Cuxa, Bonnefont, and Trie – had been brought from Europe. The stones and decorative elements had been rearranged and reconstructed to create something like an original-reproduction, not a bad analogy for certain kinds of writing (Bonnie Young, *A Walk Through the Cloisters*).

But I didn't really discover the atmosphere and essence for me of the Cloisters until a fateful period at the end of my first year of high school when I began to read seriously: Somerset Maugham's *Of Human Bondage;* Samuel Butler's *The Way of All Flesh;* Thomas Mann's *Buddenbrooks;* Thomas Wolfe's *Look Homeward, Angel;* Fitzgerald's *Tender Is the Night;* Hemingway's *The Sun Also Rises;* the poetry of T. S. Eliot. These works in a variety of ways led me to an interest in "Art" (with a capital "A") and to the origin and development of Art in Western Culture (an interest in other cultures would come later). I wanted to go to Jerusalem; I wanted to see Athens and Rome. I wanted to see the famous windows at Chartres. I wanted to stand on the parapets (if that was possible) of Hamlet's castle in Denmark. I wanted to sail to Byzantium and did, later, when I spent a year in Turkey.

I discovered that medieval music was played in the Cloisters on Sunday mornings, and I would go there sometimes, dreamily immersed in one of the books I was reading, moved by the monkish music, convinced that I would find myself, when I put the book down, in some far-away and remote place, not unlike the setting of the particular book that I happened to be reading. Books became a form of travel. As Keats says famously in "On First Looking into Chapman's Homer":

> Much have I travell'd in realms of gold,
> And many goodly states and kingdoms seen;
> Round many western islands have I been
> Which bards in fealty to Apollo hold.

And I came to understand, or believe, that most writers had to travel in order to write. Sea voyages held together writers who had little else in common: Homer and Jack London; Somerset Maugham and the anonymous author of the Old English "Seafarer." The author of *The Gentleman in the Parlour* had little in common with the singer who "weathered the winter, wretched outcast/Deprived of my kinsmen" (Pound 207), but they were fellow voyagers: going out into the great world for material; recreating that world in "tranquility" (Wordsworth). Imagining a world and then looking for it. Lord Francis Bacon understood in the sixteenth century the connection between travel and writing in his "Of Travel."

> It is a strange thing that, in sea-voyages, where there is nothing to be seen but sky and sea, men should make diaries; but in land travel, wherein so much is to be observed, for the most part they omit it: as if chance were fitter to be registered than observation. Let diaries, therefore, be brought in use. (Bacon 72)

Lord Bacon inaugurates an age of autobiography and other forms of personal writing: travel-observe-absorb-write (in the first person, if you wish). Like Montaigne before him and the wonderful Romantic British essayists after (Hazlitt, Lamb), Bacon believed that personal observations could become general truths.

Those special moments and hours in the Cloisters soon gave way to a fascination with Paris in the 1920s. I read as many memoirs of the period as I could, Malcolm Cowley's *Exile's Return,* among them. It seemed that just about all American writers of any significance had had their Paris experience. There were other ports of literary call, including New York's own Greenwich Village, London, Rome, Tangiers; but Paris seemed to be where the main action was. Since I had made up by mind by age seventeen to become some kind of American writer, I knew I had to get to Paris.

If you couldn't sit at a cafe with a Gitanes dangling from your lower lip, chatting about existential books over the clatter of espresso cups, you didn't stand a chance of getting to the top of Mount Parnassus, or even having a glimpse of the peak. There were, of course, French restaurants in New York, some even famous, such as Chambord, where my father once took me before he went broke. Its sepia-toned front window, subdued lighting, and simple elegance whispered to me subliminally that there was much in the world that I hadn't yet seen. And some coffee houses were springing up in the postwar Europeanization of America, the Coffee Mill, for one. And the, yes, Paris Theatre on West 56th Street, just off Fifth Avenue, served espresso in its banquette-lined lounge. But it wasn't Paris with a capital "P." And even though Paris, Illinois, has a capital "P," that wasn't Paris either.

And there were some French movies, at the Paris and a few other places. If you were an adolescent interested in anything like a frank representation of love and sex in those days, you had to read *National Geographic* or go to French movies. I assumed in some sense that you had to speak French or be an anthropologist in order to have an intimate relationship. In brief, I believed that you had to go to France in order to be in briefs with a partner in an erotic setting. But how was I going to get to Europe? My father, poor guy, down on his luck, was having a hard enough time keeping me in college.

My father's pinched circumstances and a very modest academic salary made it almost impossible for me to travel widely for many years. For a long time, more affluent Buffalo colleagues from The State University of New York at Buffalo (SUNY at Buffalo) would travel far and wide in the summer, and I jokingly, self-mocking, would say, "Bon voyage, I hope to see more of the Erie Canal." But the delay whetted my appetite further to go out into the great world.

I had come to believe, growing up, that place and atmosphere, that sites and their spatial setting were crucial determinants in a writer's development. I had come to believe, without thinking much about it, that architecture and the density of decorative elements in old villages and cities were stimulants for the imagination. As you needed aromatic coffee in the morning to get started, so you needed a good view – something I still believe in. It's always been possible to have the coffee. The view has been harder. I have had to travel for that. I looked into the bowl of central Ankara from my terrace in Cankaya and across glittering "fragrant harbour" to Kowloon from another terrace in Hong Kong.

If you wanted to write, you needed to be surrounded by what Henry James calls in "The Art of Fiction" (1884) "solidity of specification," and a lot of that gravity rested on European ground (some of it in ruins): walls in holes. I wasn't aware at the time of Henry James's famous remarks about Hawthorne, but I agree with him when he says: "It takes such an accumulation of history and custom, such a complexity of manners and types, to form a fund of suggestion for a novelist." To say nothing of "thatched cottages" or "little Norman churches" (Henry James 60). I would come to see later that every family is, in one way or another, deep and complex, an impasto of memory as thick as a historic monument. One doesn't need necessarily to travel to traverse continents of consciousness or to scale Pater's "thick wall" of personality" as he says at the conclusion of his *The Renaissance*.

My chance for the Grand Tour and *wanderjahre* came during 1956–57 when a late uncle of mine who lived in a state of permanent psychological exile (the diaspora of his soul), later a suicide, asked me if I would be his chauffeur and companion for a year in Europe. Without knowing much else about the deal, I accepted, took a year's leave of absence from Amherst College, and flew to Copenhagen, our first meeting place, via (pre-jet) Gander (Newfoundland), Shannon, and Paris. It broke my heart to see the roofs of Paris appear and disappear on the way in and out as I was in transit, but I knew I would get back to them after a few months in Scandinavia and Britain. And when I did I meet Hemingway at the Ritz Bar in Paris, he told me, belting down a double scotch (Chivas), that he was going to hunt pheasant in Spain in a few days. I thought of the fowl in Fort Tryon Park and wanted to stop him, but said nothing. He was Hemingway. He shot himself a few years later. I should have said something.

And I did get back to Paris at the end of the summer when I sat at one of the Left Bank's fabled existential cafe's in Montparnasse and wrote letters home to my Amherst College friends. It was in writing these first letters from Europe that I discovered the double nature of travel writing or writing about travel. In leaving home and writing about it to friends and family (to say nothing of other kinds of writing that one might do overseas), one inevitably revisits home.

As I sat in what Hemingway calls in *A Moveable Feast* a "good cafe," I thought of a song that was popular at my college at that time, "Long Ago and Far-Away." If I might have thought then that the "long ago" (one's childhood and youth) was "far-away" (at a temporal distance), I might say today that one is torn always between the claims of the past and the allure of that which is geographically far away. Or both sets of feeling may be at work at the same time. By the way, the hyphen is meaningful: "far-away" is dreamy; "far away" suggests distance. Once you have been somewhere and had your passport stamped, it is no longer an exotic place, the site of daydreams. One's card of identity becomes part of one's identity.

One possibly sees home for the first time in a fresh light in leaving it and, finally, in returning in some fashion; and most people do come home, even after decades. Knowledge is always contrastive. One sets this evidence against that data, this pattern against that framework; and nothing could be more contrastive than what I might call "lived cultural anthropology." In penning those first letters and affixing those first French stamps in the pre-computer era, I had a sense of – what an Indian writer in Hyderabad called many years later – "international drama." I felt the need to reconnect with a lost world, even as I was beginning to discover a new one. Nothing binds as closely as the ties of one's original home; and no tether needs to be broken more decisively. It may be that we can preserve this doubleness of our existence only in and through writing. For this reason, I titled a book of travel letters some years ago *A Version of Home: Letters from the World.*

Although I had grown up in New York City and had seen the cityscape of Lower Manhattan from the railing of a Staten Island ferry, had seen it from the promenade in Brooklyn Heights, had seen it from the observation deck of the Empire State Building (once again, after 9/11, the tallest building in New York City), I never had seen it as I would come to see it at dawn when I sailed home on the *Queen Elizabeth* through the eyes of a young man who had been away from home for a year.

F. Scott Fitzgerald says in "My Lost City" (23): "There was first the ferry boat moving softly from the Jersey shore at dawn – the moment crystallized into my first symbol of New York. ... The ferry boat stood for triumph, the girl for romance." New York seemed to me to be monumentally a fact and symbol of Home and, it struck me, Homeland. I felt – as the great ship eased past the Statue of Liberty and Ellis Island, churning through New York harbor toward the mouth of the Hudson

River – some of the awe that my paternal grandfather, a Lithuanian immigrant, and my mother's father, a Czech, must have felt when they arrived by ship in New York City in the first decade of the twentieth century.

In flight from poverty and oppression, they had come to America in search of a "new life." I, an overly protected and privileged child of the slightly upper middle class, had gone to Europe to seek adventure, culture, and the increased freedom that would make writing a possibility. I now returned with the sense that New York was more than my home. The Statue of Liberty had been and remained (at least until September 11, 2001) "the Mother of Exiles," a haven for the "homeless." The cliche, now emotionally charged, had become an archetype. After 9/11, New York would never look quite as safe. After 9/11, America would look suspiciously, even paranoically, at the world and might act rashly toward "strangers." It has.

This sense of New York came back to me when I was working on a novel in 1981 that eventually appeared in 1996 (a story in itself with stops in Buffalo; Charleston, South Carolina; Sweet Briar, Virginia; and Hong Kong). There is a scene in this somewhat fanciful novel, *Broadway Serenade,* in which the reluctant hero imagines himself hang gliding with Dacron wings over Manhattan and having an overview of his family's history in America (138–139):

> If he didn't have such a fear of the vertical, he would relive the movement of his family north through almost a century on Manhattan. He could join the immigrant trek through the veldts of Manhattan until his family had arrived in Washington Heights. He might discover the meaning of his origins.... He could join his grandfather, foot-peddler in the New Land, and see what lay before and below him.

And the novel moves toward a conclusion in Fort Tryon Park (209):

> Larry turned up his collar and made his way along
> the paths, down the steps, over and around parapets,
> on his way to the Cloisters which he could see against
> the background of a Northern sky, sitting on the
> highest point of Manhattan like a 12th Century
> fortress: one of the dominant images of his childhood....

Had I not gone overseas, had I not spent a difficult year with
my late uncle, I would not have returned to New York and
America with an altered vision of its reality for me, at once
more and less European: far removed from the seedbed of art
and culture (just to touch on one issue); forever recreating that
legacy in new terms, as the Cloisters itself was a recreation; at
once far removed from the sacred origins of belief, the only
safe haven of belief for people of many lands.

Had I not gone to Europe after two years of college, I
would not have been able to set the facts and patterns of my
life up to that point in the context of new facts and patterns. I
wouldn't have understood my father's relation to his older
brother; I wouldn't have known how much my college and
college friends meant to me; I wouldn't have seen the
devastating impact of the war on Europe's cities and civilian
populations. One wants to put the isolated object of personal
experience and consciousness of experience in the context of
nothing less than the entire world.

We do not have to travel in order to go through this
imaginative and cognitive process, but it helps. Nothing is more
persuasive than the difference, say, between the scent of Hong
Kong and the aroma of Buffalo. And one needn't go anywhere
in a spatial sense to enter new worlds. As Thoreau says in
Walden (6): "Could a greater miracle take place than for us to
look through each other's eyes for an instant? We should live
in all the ages of the world in an hour; ay, in all the world of
the ages."

But it isn't so easy to enter another person's mind or to
share the minute variations of awareness with another person.

It is easier and more dramatic to begin with one's outer journeys, with a description of far-away places, as a prelude to an exploration of inner worlds. The greatest writers can put the two worlds together: Henry James, James Joyce, Virginia Woolf, D. H. Lawrence, Richard Wright, Isaac Bashevis Singer, Nadine Gordimer. In many ways, writing itself is an act of voyage and discovery, as old-fashioned as this may sound. Writing gives you a chance to arrange yourself in relation to the world.

Re-vision

I didn't realize when I went to Europe in 1956-57 with a late uncle (an anguished widower looking for a new home, a suicide eventually), that I was beginning a reversal of my American history in familial and cultural terms. My grandfathers and grandmothers had barely escaped the perils of poverty and marginal lives in pre-Nazi Europe, and I would return at some point to give a lecture in Germany. It was, ironically, a small legacy from this uncle that allowed me to buy a modest home, but a home, in Buffalo's nearest suburb, the town of Amherst.

My grandparents, who could tell me very little about their pasts because they didn't speak English well and who may have known little because they were denied education, would have been surprised, and perhaps appalled, that I, who had grown up exclusively in the apparent safety of America, would choose to live two years of my life in mainly Moslem countries – Turkey and Malaysia. They had risked everything to get to New York City, the imagined reinvention of the "promised land," the Lower East Side of Manhattan as a version, however shabby, of the New Jerusalem.

Why then would I give up the comfort zone of a place where the Sabbath could be observed safely in the sanctity of a home that enjoyed all the protection of American law? The short answer is that I was more interested in observing life beyond the safe boundaries that my parents' generation made possible for me than I was in being observant in a traditional sense. Longer and more complex reasons are explored and discovered in the next and following chapters into the pastness of the present and the presentness of the past, or perhaps I should say the presentiments of the past.

CHAPTER TWO

WAGNER'S SHED:
PROPERTY AND FANTASY IN THE AMERICAN BACKYARD

W ho was Wagner, and what was in his shed and yard? Was it possible that someone so ornery and obsessive could teach me anything about America at this late date in the twentieth century? Did it make any sense to think that "old man Wagner" – as the neighbors called him – could tell me anything I didn't already know about my life and country? America was, after all, in its fourth period of exploration) the discovery of the land, westward expansion, the discovery of self, and now space travel. What could Wagner add?

It seemed unlikely that old man Wagner, a chip off the strata of the Niagara escarpment of western New York State, an octogenarian shard, could help me uncover any new truths. But I was interested in him. He was an old bird, and I became a bird watcher from the moment I rented a renovated carriage house on Richmond Avenue near Buffalo's lower West Side: a melting pot of old WASP (White Anglo-Saxon Protestant), emergent Italian middle class, blue-collar, and falling (if not quite fallen) academic.

I became fascinated with Wagner when I noticed the fortifications and parapets of debris built along the line of the fence joining his house and mine. I didn't understand how he could so brazenly let the weight of his wood and metal hoard push against the fence and begin to cave it in. Wagner was violating several codes – official and unofficial, legal and social – and was getting away with it in somewhat rural America where property lines and boundaries are clearer than in the big city.

It didn't make any sense, and I was determined to find out what Wagner was up to. I would try to force him to get his stuff off the fence and haul it away from the side of the house where his junk-works and rusting road-signs whistled, hummed, and flapped in the windy night like musical saws. His NO EXIT was the leader of the band.

But first I wanted to find out what Wagner was about. He was a survivor of one sort or another, I surmised, and I might learn something from him. If nothing else, he had made it through more than a half-century of Buffalo winters and had come through two wars in which he might have served. He had outlived aloneness and, doubtless, loneliness. He was a man without family, cut off from the family of man.

It might have been easier just to ask him and get it over with. But, even though there weren't many manners left in America to which people subscribed uniformly, it still wasn't quite permissible to walk up to someone and ask, flat out, "Why are you nuts?" Americans had gotten used to doing just about everything in public in the aftermath of the 1960s and had been extending the claims of Emersonian self-expression for a century and a half (with technology and communication systems making the exposing of the psyche easier all the time); but there were still a few residual decencies and cordial echoes that held me back from asking the intrusive truth about a man to his face.

At first Wagner's movements and collection habits seemed random, even as I suspected they weren't, and it soon became clear that Wagner surveyed his nocturnal acquisitions during the day as he made the rounds of his dilapidated house, trimming an odd hedge here or there. If he seemed to others always to be doing the same thing – walking stoop-shouldered through the neighborhood with his hobnailed stick – I could see that he was involved in a careful sorting process.

These special items included broken toys, especially wooden ones; pre-Second World War tin signs; latticework and hitching-post rings from the turn of the century; leaded glass sections; carved ornamental filigree from one or another abandoned nineteenth-century mansion in the neighborhood; oak planks and beams; marbles and polished stone. It was a collection, not just an assortment of dead objects. He was seemingly as driven to collect his things as Wall Street investors to accumulate wealth or the new entrepreneurs to outfit a sailboat.

Wagner parodied the urge to acquire and fortify, to amass and store. He didn't so much have the Midas touch as he had a few Midas mufflers; but, as I looked at things, his things, him, over the fence, he didn't seem to be so different from, or more unpleasant than, the upper crust and would-be pretenders to the privileged life. Wagner worked furtively in much the same way that the great American entrepreneurs of the nineteenth century had operated: grabbing everything in sight when no one was looking. As R. H. Tawney says in *The Acquisitive Society*, "The lords of the jungle do not hunt by daylight."

For all I knew, Wagner had been to the manner born (maybe he even *had* been born in the Birge manor across the street, originally the home of the wallpaper company owner for whom the American artist Charles Burchfield worked) and was serving the aspirations and tastes – however meretricious – of a better and more coherent past. Who knew who he was really? Maybe he was a fossil descendant of one of Buffalo's original and established families.

It might make as much sense to apply social and economic categories to Wagner as it would to study the demise of Bethlehem Steel and the loss of business to Japan. It was possible to look at Wagner as a microcosm and analogue of larger forces of accumulation. From this point of view, Wagner's movements were as mysterious as the fluctuations of the stock market and the ebb and flow of money around the world through the Exchanges of New York and Hong Kong. But he did more than merely pile and hoard like a miser and precious metal speculator. He concealed and arranged, and, in this way, he could be thought of as a jewel maker, archaeologist, and paleontologist. I could see that he used junk as a decoy, that he hid, as it were, in the blind of his own debris. Closer observation revealed that Wagner had built something like a miniature city of earthworks – possibly a network of cities, possibly a civilization – whose meaning was obscure, but whose icons, shrines, and crossroads were there for anyone – for anyone who cared about such obscurities – to observe.

If these comparisons didn't fit exactly, they served as a counterbalance to the more obvious charges that one was likely to bring against him. As I took stock of my life, and wondered about America, on the verge of leaving the country for a year on a Fulbright, the beginning, as it turned out, of a two-decade circumnavigation, I became more attentive to the daily activities of my countryman and native land. Wagner was giving me a chance, without knowing it, to find out more about myself and my mysterious homeland where the blend of fact and fantasy (including empiric ideology) vex the imagination and may end up being the country's undoing.

It wasn't clear if Wagner was building an alternate world out of the discards and wreckage of his life as an act of homage, sacrilege, or even as his own defense against an imagined thermonuclear attack; but he certainly had been at work for decades. I wanted to understand what Wagner was building. I even thought of taking photographs of his work with a concealed camera, but I was wary of the possible uses of his hob-nailed stick, and I didn't want to drive him indoors permanently. I feared his potential threat to himself and me.

People, even some I knew, might choose to be electronic shut-ins, as I called them, but I didn't want to drive another nail into Wagner's already largely boarded-up house. So, I had to snoop cautiously and choose opportune times to investigate his ruins. I saw on these occasions, or when I took out the trash and garbage and peered through the slate of Wagner's rear fence, that he had scoured the neighborhood for talismanic collectibles, that he had gathered bits and pieces of the city's discards and begun to rework them after the brilliant shadow-box artist Joseph Cornell into an anti-world. He worked as a collagist or assemblagist to construct the present out of the past, to reconstruct the past.

In the American provinces, far from the centers of contemporary taste, Wagner had managed, somehow, to take on the leading attitudes of Modernism. Doubtless ignorant of T. S. Eliot, Freud, and Picasso, he had felt in his old bones the need to preserve the past by finding the objective equivalents of feeling and hammering them into some kind of permanent form of nostalgia. He differed from the modern masters mainly in his failure of self-consciousness. He was an artist of sorts, or we could say that the symptomatic expression of his inner life, the objective terms in which he revealed himself and showed himself to the world, went beyond the usual array of tics and mannerisms that usually characterize people who can't express themselves as well as artists.

His world, if I may call it that, presented itself concretely as a midpoint between art and pathology. His mounds and burrows seemed to be publicly meaningful, but weren't; they seemed to be aesthetically pleasing, but added up seemingly to nothing. Neither a grotesque nor an artist, he moved through his own hidden designs. I needed to shed more light on the subject, though, and rigged up a makeshift light on the side of my rented house. It was possible, of course, that the light might drive Wagner out of the corners of the night, but I was racing against the clock to find out something important about America and the West before I entered the Mediterranean and

Islamic worlds, before I set out to see a larger world than the one I had lived in since I came to The State University of New York at Buffalo as a young assistant professor of English.

Wagner's shed might hold some clues to the life I had led. Was it possible, for instance, that Wagner could teach me how and why family bonds and tribal compassion could be displaced by the desire and need to acquire matter and money?

I didn't much change my habits and routines, I listened carefully and attentively as I read at night and hoped that I would hear Wagner's footsteps, the scraping or crackling of some object, and catch him in the middle of bagging a fragment. But the nocturnal shuffling had stopped. I seemed to have put an end to Wagner's wanderings. I wondered if I had been wise, even if I had been cruel, if I had destroyed the very evidence that I wanted.

I had pretty much given up the hope of discovering any more about him when I heard a tapping and hammering on the side of the house one morning a few days later. I thought at first that a family of woodpeckers had joined the cardinals in the backyard I now thought of as a bower, but even I — a son of Manhattan — realized instantly that no woodpecker could make that kind of assault upon the house. I drew aside the curtain. It was old man Wagner on a stepladder, whacking away at the clapboard. I stared in disbelief as Wagner – the embodiment of property and property values, of proprietary relationships – struck the metal plate of the floodlight. If he had stood for anything, it was hoarding and privacy. What did he think he was doing attacking the side of *my* house?

"Wagner! What are you doing?"

"Just fixing this light for you," he said, tremulously.

"Hell you are," I growled, "you're destroying my property. Get the hell off the side of my house."

"Just trying to be helpful," Wagner said. "Just trying to put the light at a better angle."

"Some chance, get off my house."

"Isn't your house anyway," he said, "you're just a renter."

"You just take care of your junk, I'll take care of mine."

"Isn't junk."

"Whatever."

"Just being neighborly."

"First time," I said.

"Just wanted to get you a better angle to the back. You never know who's out there at night."

"Put a light on the side of your house."

"Just being neighborly;" he said, as he stepped off the ladder, folded it, and slumped toward the shed where he seemed to keep the tools he used for collecting, arranging, and storing his hoard.

Maybe he was telling the truth. Maybe I had missed an opportunity to decipher the Rosetta stone and Linear A & B of Wagner's life, but I didn't think so. I would have bet anything that the old man was lying to me, as well as to himself, but it didn't make a difference. Wagner hadn't earned the right to come onto my property. If he had made a life out of the difference between his material world and the world of others, if his house and property defined the distinction between self and other, then I couldn't just let him cross the line without some ritualistic and compensatory gestures.

Then Wagner's lights went out, and he disappeared. I thought that I would never see him again or ever come to see the inside of his mind and house (were they different?) before I left for Ankara and the treeless plain of Central Anatolia where I would teach for a year at Ankara University as a Fulbright Lecturer. I felt some sadness about this, but thought we probably had come through the floodlight incident with as little mayhem as possible. So far as he knew, I was just annoyed with him. He knew nothing about my inner drama as I knew really nothing about his. He was probably sulking, nothing worse.

I was ready to accept responsibility for what I had done as I left the house a few nights later to wait for a taxi to take me to the airport for an evening flight to New York, the first leg of my journey to Turkey. I sat on the stoop of the house facing the street in front of my carriage house and tried to imagine the inside of Wagner's house. A taxi approached, its lights flooding me.

It was as if the frame of his house – shrouded in darkness, illumined by the occasional glimmer of a low-wattage bulb or chalky flicker of an ancient black-and-white TV set (doubtless one he had picked off the street) – were suddenly ignited in flame, casting a glow inward, so that all the levels, like a doll house, were visible.

I saw, in this incandescent moment, that the rooms were filled with scraps and pieces of wood and metal, except for the gabled attic, which was elegantly decorated and appointed in something like the style of the Regency Period. I thought I could see what looked like an escritoire, hutch, and spinet of the period just after the American Revolution. I saw, in my mind's eye, that Wagner's *Walpurgisnacht*, the flame of his life, would reveal the remnant of a late neoclassic dream. He was trying, perhaps, to build a dream of a more civilized America out of the broken pieces, as he took it, of the present. It was, of course, a task that could only lead to one sort of ruin or another; or if it did not lead to ruin, his kind of nocturnal salvage act, his theme park, could lead to an inability to live in the present, an unwillingness to reach across a fence to lend a helping hand to a neighbor.

Still, as the fire raged in my mind, I couldn't help feel a kind of grudging respect for Wagner and what he may have taught me about my country in its desperate effort to replace history with fantasy in the absence of family coherence. He had taught me something about the risk of not living with others in the present.

"Call a cab, mister?"

As I saw his house outlined against the sky, I thought I saw him, too, standing on his porch conducting some unheard music. He seemed, in that instant, less threatened by flames then he did transfigured by light.

"Cab, mister?"

I thought I heard a Sousa march and some measures of a Charles Ives symphony. Wagner was possibly trying, as I imagined him, to tell me something about the difficulty of being alone in America in the electronic era, or maybe he was just confused again, trying to put together pieces that couldn't be joined.

"Just wait a few weeks," he seemed to mouth, "you'll learn something about the pain of old and new, then you'll have more respect for old man Wagner. Wait until Ankara, wait until Hong Kong, you'll see, you'll learn something about family and history."

The light faded. The house was dark again.

"Okay, cabbie."

It was time to go.

I thought of Wagner in Turkey months later when I came across a passage in a letter from Edmund Wilson to F. Scott Fitzgerald (July 5, 1921, *Portable Wilson*):

> America seems to be actually beginning to express herself in something like an idiom of her own. But, believe me, she has a long way to go. The commercialism and industrialism, with no older and more civilized civilization behind except one layer of eighteenth century of the East Coast, impose a terrific handicap...

Wagner and I were brothers of sorts, as it turned out, as I came to see. We both had lost touch with our family origins. In the absence of family, we each had turned to versions of history that became fantasy: his as a collection of broken objects, mine as an attempt to make a story out of his and my life, a story that would take me out into the far reaches of the Great World in the years to come.

We would have done better to become good neighbors and build from there, but too much came between us – city-country, generational differences, and the phobic property line. Still, I vowed to myself that when I returned from Anatolia that I would buy a house – what else could I do in a country where reality and real estate were almost equivalent terms? – And try nonetheless to cross the fence, to reach out and try to know a neighbor.

If the family were in chaos and history running amok, it made sense to get to know a neighbor instead of making up a story about him or her. At least I would give it a try one day. I wanted to think that it might be possible to substitute transparency for privacy; to imagine a day when "men will no longer have secrets from each other" as Sartre suggests ("Self-Portrait at Seventy" in *Life/Situations*), "because subjective life, as well as objective life, will be completely offered up, given." If these would be dreamy thoughts, looking across the Bosporus from Europe to Asia, they were also useful reminders of a world one might strive for.

Re-vision

I didn't know when I bid farewell to Wagner's poor estate at the beginning of my journey to Turkey that I would return to America a year later as a somewhat transformed person, an international man, so to speak, a person committed to Internationalism. Nor did I know that my immersion in a version of Islamic life in post-Ataturk Turkey would prefigure in some ways the increased importance of the Moslem world in the geo-politics of the late twentieth and early twenty-first centuries.

But I can see now, the meaning of "re-vision," after all, that I had a longing for belonging to a community that went beyond the boundaries of Buffalo, Erie County, New York, a Great Lake port-city and region that history and trade sadly had left behind. The most visible legacy of once viable Native American "nations" was now gambling casinos. I see as well that the academic life I had led from 1967 to 1983, the time of my departure for Turkey and the beginning of my new life as an overseas teacher and lecturer (as well as someone who would write about and out of these experiences), had not provided me with a profound sense of social cohesion.

The dynamic and, in some sense, communal, spirit of the anti-Vietnam War years on university campuses had created the impression that America was moving closer to something like a utopian notion of brotherhood and sisterhood, the family of man. But when the Vietnam War ended, mercifully, in 1975, leaving 58,229 men dead in the ditch of the disaster, it became increasingly clear that some of the positive gains had been all too temporary and illusory. University departments, like mine, which had been galvanized into some kind of solidarity with students who might fight and die in far-away rice paddies, returned to research as usual, with more attention than ever paid to government funding.

Starting with Turkey, I began to put together and to compose an international community of friends and colleagues, who would, in the fullness of time, make up for me a world at once symbolic and palpable. Here today, but gone tomorrow. If I was an outsider in some ways, I had found other outsiders who equally craved a sense of connection with a world larger and less divisive than the ones in which they lived. This would prove to be one of the unifying terms of my travel experiences: a coming together and bonding of strangers in the night-train of dislocation.

CHAPTER THREE

BLUEPRINT FOR A CHANGING WORLD: SOME ROLES OF AMERICAN STUDIES OVERSEAS TODAY

*A*s a sophomore at Amherst College in 1955–56, when I was required to take an American Studies course, I was interested in the "Problems of Civilization" that we were asked to consider and write about: *The New Deal: Revolution or Evolution? The Meaning of Jacksonian Democracy, Slavery as a Cause of the Civil War* (cf. Bate and Frank). But I was more interested *then* in English literature. I did not think of myself as a student of American literature and culture until I had a small awakening one day on a bus in New York City a few years later, when it occurred to me that I could never know as much about the literature of Britain as I could about the literature of my own country.

I agreed with T. S. Eliot in his "Tradition and the Individual Talent" that the "historical sense" requires us first to write with our "own generation" in our "bones," but I knew that my bones were American as I looked at the majestic Hudson River as the bus headed south from my neighborhood, Washington Heights, to Morningside Heights and Columbia University: landscapes of the early Republic. As the grandson of Lithuanian immigrants on my father's side and Czech immigrants on my mother's, I felt a sense of gratitude to America for giving my family a homeland; and I was determined *then* to become as American as I could be.

Exile and expatriation were privileges; it seemed to me, of the landed and established, the sons and daughters of the American Revolution, the highly gifted, and the oppressed (Henry James, Ernest Hemingway, Richard Wright). Besides, America had just spearheaded an Allied victory over Germany and Japan: its Flying Fortresses had dominated the skies; its young men had shed blood on foreign soil to protect the Wilsonian legacy of self-determination, the basic tenets of constitutional democracy, and international law. It was, in the words of Henry Luce, "the American Century" (Brogan 606). "Why," I asked myself on that fateful bus ride downtown, "would I want to study English literature at a time when 'The Star-Spangled Banner' was replacing 'God Save the Queen' as an inspiring anthem for nations emerging from the ruins of fascism, war, genocide, and holocaust?"

I have no doubt, looking back, that my incidental revelation was part of a larger impulse – both in America and overseas – to recognize the importance, the empiric status really, of America in the immediate post World War II period. I felt and understood at a personal level a change that was taking place in the world at that time; the Americanization of Europe and parts of Asia, a shift from a British and Euro dominated world (with its legacy of colonial rule) to one of American economic and cultural hegemony (particularly in the area of popular culture: blue jeans and James Dean). President Truman's signing of the Fulbright Act on August 1, 1946, the U.S. Information and Educational Exchange Act of 1948, and the Fulbright-Hays Act of 1961 (*Terms and Conditions* 1993, ii) were at once symbols of America's new cultural and educational role in world affairs and political attempts (largely successful) to expand that role. American Studies and the study of American civilization came of age in the post-Hiroshima and post-Yalta period as an expression of America's confidence in itself (its institutions and way of life), its desire to spread its influence, and as part of the world's recognition that it was important and perhaps even beneficial to understand something about the new world: its democratic political stability, technological sophistication, and educational excellence; its expanding markets (domestic and international), efficiency, imagination, and openness.

The study of American literature and culture advanced inevitably a view of America that was consistent with America's new role in world affairs. Indeed, the idea of America's relative "newness" and related ideas were set against Europe's "oldness" and obsolescence in the aftermath of World War II. Myths of innocence and origin were in the air. Its critics and historians described America as a "virgin land" and "second Eden"; the "frontier," as *interpreted* by Frederick Jackson Turner in his famous "The Significance of the Frontier in American History," became the crucible of liberal democracy. The emergence of American Studies (and, within it, or next to it, the study of American literature) was part of the celebration of American-style democracy after V-E and V-J Days, after the defeat of two ultra-nationalist states that had been committed, in one form or other, to ethnic and racial "purity."

America celebrated its immigrant legacy and the apparent success of the "melting pot" in this post-war period; and *E Pluribus Unum* (held firmly in the teeth of the eagle) became, in effect, the national motto. Those of us who were attending lectures in Amherst's College Hall (itself an emblem of mid-nineteenth-century righteousness) did not doubt that we would participate in a life of discovery and expansion that would replicate, in some way, Whitman's celebration in "Passage to India" of Columbus's voyage.

> The mediaeval navigators rise before me,
> The world of 1492, with its awaken'd enterprise,
> Something swelling in humanity now like the sap
> Of the earth in spring,
> The sunset splendor of chivalry declining.

And who art thou sad shade?
Gigantic, visionary, thyself a visionary,
With majestic limbs and pious beaming eyes,
Spreading around with every look of thine a
Golden world,
Enhuing it with gorgeous hues. (16)

If we had reservations about the promises of the post-war boom (and we did, of course), they took the form of apprehensions about giving up individuality and selfhood in the name of corporate enterprise and a pre-established, assigned family destiny; but we did not doubt that our rebellion against the nuclear family (a microcosm of the society as a whole) would lead to some kind of creative self-realization.

The movies, plays, and prose of the period (family drama) supported this view: *Death of a Salesman, A Streetcar Named Desire, Rebel Without a Cause, The Catcher in the Rye, The Member of the Wedding,* to give a few examples. This sense of what I recently have come to call "creative alienation" was reinforced by the monumental importance given to Mark Twain's *The Adventures of Huckleberry Finn* by the leading American critics of the post-war era. Their celebration of Huck Finn combined what was still viable of the 1930s legacy *after* the Hitler-Stalin Pact of 1939 (the betrayal of the Left) with a positive reading of escapist tendencies, especially as those figures representing a movement from restraint toward freedom were associated with the American West. This was a quiet, but deep, resistance on the part of my 1950s contemporaries to the self-congratulatory tendencies of America in the post-war period; and it reflected, as well, the influence of Freud and psychoanalysis, a spin-off, we might say, of the Nazi era, the immigration of displaced academics and intellectuals to the United States as refugees and survivors. But this resistance did not seriously challenge and call into question America's role in the post-war period. Even the "Beat" movement, the most obvious cultural challenge to

America in the pre-Vietnam era, was only a blip on the national radar screen; and Jack Kerouac's *On the Road* did not so much threaten America's middle class as titillate it. And the Beats were in their way celebrating what they took to be America's greatest legacy – freedom, though they didn't really define it or state its limits.

Needless to say, a great deal has changed in America and the world since my undergraduate days. To be a successful American no longer means exclusively, as it did for my generation, to cultivate a White Anglo-Saxon Protestant (WASP) lifestyle: to enter the Halls of Ivy and the canyons of Wall Street (cf. Pfaff). America is now a much more multiracial, multiethnic, and multinational society. We might even say that it is more powerful, relative to the world, in the wake of the collapse of the former Soviet Union and the Gulf War, but this is no longer a sufficient index of national greatness at the end of the twentieth century.

In a real sense, America and the Soviet Union created (and exaggerated) each other's stature during the period of the Cold War. The Cold War served to conceal (or override) national weaknesses; and its demise leaves each side with its weaknesses exposed, the former Soviet Union more damaged than any Soviet hand or Kremlinologist could have predicted; the U.S. uncertain about its hegemonic status as empire: whether it possesses it, whether it wants to possess it (uncertain about how to act in either case).

Despite the first George Bush's efforts to assert a New World Order at the end of the Gulf War in the eleventh hour of his presidency, with America in the cockpit, everyone (including the American voting public) knew that America needed more to compete and cooperate in economic terms on a global scale than it needed to dominate militarily. America needed, first, to balance its budget and correct its imbalance of trade; and it could not attend to these items without reducing the cost of its military. The end of the Cold War makes America both more and less powerful: more powerful than its old adversary, but less necessary as a mega-power in the world. Other wealthy nations can rush in where angels fear to tread, particularly Germany and Japan, once their governments sort out appropriate military missions in the post Cold War era. These tortuous efforts of national self-definition have been going on for several decades.

The rising European (EU) and Asian economies (especially Germany and Japan, along with the Dragons) over the past two decades have been the most powerful forces affecting America's perception of itself as well as the world's perception of America. Where my generation saw the Americanization of Europe and parts of Asia, the present generation sees the Asianization and Hispanicization of America in terms at once observable and atmospheric.

Even as overseas students flock to America for advanced training, they recognize that they bring, in the main, more discipline and a stronger work ethic with them; they recognize that they are taking more advantage of America's advanced educational opportunities, especially at the postgraduate level in the areas of science and technology, than Americans themselves, and they believe as well (I have heard many such opinions in Hong Kong) that better opportunities await them at home once they have "returned" and that, furthermore, they find American society and culture to be often incoherent and violent.

The destruction of the Branch Davidians in Waco, Texas, for example establishes America, once again, as a country where the forces of law and lawlessness act out a scenario of fantasy and violence that transgresses the boundaries of reason; and these distortions compromise our good name and damage our image as it is transmitted worldwide (CNN, BBC World Service). Visitors are puzzled also by the apparent illiteracy and innumeracy of a country that is, in fact, training them at the highest levels in physics, medicine, engineering, and other technical fields. These students (and America-watchers) may fail to understand that "falling" standards in the lower grades and high schools are a consequence (perhaps a temporary one) precisely of America's effort (however ambivalent in some cases) to absorb new populations, new languages, new perceptions of learning itself.

As much as anything and in ways that still defy full comprehension, the Vietnam War changed America's perception of itself more really than the world's perception of America. If America "lost" the war, it was a loss everyone understood. It was a matter of will rather than might; and I would say that it was precisely the "loss" in Vietnam that led to a gain in national consciousness, a gain that offsets (potentially) many of the negatives that I have enumerated so far. It was no longer possible *after* Vietnam for Americans, including American academics, researchers, scholars, and intellectuals, to be complacent about myths of national innocence; to ignore questions of race, class, and gender. The analysis, critique, and opposition to the war in Vietnam mobilized a new generation of critics (including critics of American literature and culture) who would look closely at claims about the frontier and who would find "violence" where there had been "freedom" (Slotkin); who would find poverty where there had been affluence (Harrington); who would find the subjection of women where there had been emancipation (Gilligan, Tavris); and who would find colonialism, even alleged genocide, where there had been "discovery/encounter." The post-Vietnam era forced re-evaluations of the American experience along these lines; and a new generation of African-American scholars and scholars of African-American experience – Houston Baker Jr., John Pope Franklin, Henry L. Gates Jr., Michelle Wallace, and Eugene Genovese, to name a few – brought powerful new tools of analysis to bear upon the crippling legacy of slavery, the "peculiar institution." These progressive voices found their opposite in the post-Vietnam era in the rise of certain neo-conservative tendencies: a criticism of post-Modernist and deconstructive aesthetics *(The New Criterion);* renewed claims for the integrity of the family (cf. Broder; Wolf).

One area where America has remained substantially unchanged for my parents' generation, my generation, and the post-Vietnam and post Cold War generations is its "openness" to new immigrants; and I think that this constant of American life can provide a blueprint for change to set and correct some of the fractures that my cultural X-ray has revealed.

Even as America has lost some of its world power and some of the world's respect in certain areas, it has remained, perhaps paradoxically, a torch and beacon for poor, displaced, and oppressed peoples from all over the world: Haitians, Indians, Central Americans, Russian Jews, Vietnamese, Hong Kong Chinese, Cubans, Filipinos, and others. America remains a torch for legal and illegal immigrants because of its relative political stability, relative commitment to human rights, and openness in all spheres of life (a willingness to reinvent itself in every generation, a costly and inefficient commitment in the short run, but our best hope over the centuries), including rapid educational and economic advancement in one generation for many, if not all. These new immigrants will make even more urgent the process of cultural re-evaluation that has been under way since the 1960s, and they themselves, in what they bring to America, can provide a blueprint for change.

When Soviet President Mikhail Gorbachev and Russian President Boris Yeltsin agreed upon the dissolution of the Soviet Union in December 1991, they effectively ended the Cold War. The immediate effect was to elevate the power of the United States; but, as I have suggested, the longer-term effect has been to call for a redefinition of America in the post Cold War era. At the same time, the break-up of the Soviet Union and the subsequent ethnic-racial-territorial conflicts within the former Soviet Union and its spheres of influence (most notably Yugoslavia, Armenia, and Azerbaijan) have created a refugee problem that may constitute the world's most pressing task at the present time and which underscores the pervasive demographic displacements (willing and unwilling) of the past two decades. In helping to meet this challenge, in finding ethical and practical ways to absorb even more "foreign" populations, America can reassert its historic mission and, at the same time, reconceive that mission. At just the moment when America is haunted and shadowed by a "declinist" attitude, it can reilluminate its history by looking closely at the legacy of the Statue of Liberty, if I may be allowed to reduce this complicated set of arguments to one national symbol.

Emma Lazarus's "The New Colossus" (1883) still speaks to America's and the world's situation:

> "Keep, ancient lands, your storied pomp" cries she
> With silent lips. "Give me your tired, your poor,
> Your huddled masses yearning to breathe free,
> The wretched refuse of your teeming shore.
> Send these, the homeless, tempest-tossed to me:
> I lift my lamp beside the golden door." (480)

Although Emma Lazarus wrote this poem in response to the plight of Jews who had fled the pogroms of Russia, the poem revitalized, in time, "the old eighteenth-century idea of America as an asylum" (Higham: 480). This poem did not become immediately well known. It owes its popularity and proleptic significance largely to Louis Adamic, a Yugoslav-American author and journalist, who used the poem to launch a crusade "to elevate the status of immigrant groups and to propagate an eclectic sense of American nationality" (Primer 481). It seems appropriate at this time, almost fateful; that the popularizer of "The New Colossus" should have been Yugoslavian, for no part of the world better defines the need for the transcendence of ancient loyalties when these loyalties lead to "ethnic cleansing" and other forms of inhumanity. And we can expect that soon some of these new exiles and immigrants will look toward the "mighty woman with a torch," the "Mother of Exiles," and, when they do, I hope America will admit as many as possible with grace and intelligence.

America cannot, of course, stand alone in this effort. There needs to be an internationally funded agency (alas, another one) to gather information, demographic, resources, medical, about the displacement and movement of peoples, the possibilities for humane and economically sound resettlement. New technologies make this formidable task possible, at least at a theoretical level. As formidable as such a task may be, there is evidence (Workforce 2000 data, *Inernational Herald Tribune,* April 21, 1993) that some major economies will need, in fact to "import" people from other regions. Perhaps those who are displaced and those who seek workers can come to more harmonious terms in the future. By responding to these "endangered people" (Hoagland), America will continue to fulfill its historic mission to become, as I see it, the world's first one-world country, a blueprint for other nations.

These newest immigrants will add their cultural strengths to America's weaknesses: family coherence; the work ethic; a devotion to immediate reality; renewed discipline in the classroom (the dispossessed cannot afford to be idle); and they will insist, I hope, on preserving, within America's commitment to openness and multiplicity of belief as protected by the Constitution and other sacred Republican documents, their hyphenated identities. If they try to "melt" too willingly into the American pot, they will be reminded by critics, who came of age after the 1960s, that cultural pluralism has replaced *E Pluribus Unum* as a slogan for the 1990s. Like all slogans, it can oversimplify and serve other agendas (political correctness); but that is another matter. The newest immigrants, some of the Bosnian, Croat, and Serb children who have become "homeless," will add their voices, in time, to other new American voices; and, in so doing, they will put more pressure on America to become a truly global society. America can become, as I have suggested in this role, a model for all nations in the twenty-first century.

As economic boundaries disappear, more and more of the world's have-nots will seek their fortunes in affluent countries; and the wealthy nations will have to invest in the economies of poorer nations even as they remain willing to open their borders. As President Clinton says in his inaugural address: "To renew America, we must meet challenges abroad as well as at home. There is no longer clear division today between what is foreign and what is domestic..." (*IHT*, January 21, 1993). Some of these pressures will lead to conflict, even violence (as in the LA riots of 1992, the conflict between Koreans and African-Americans); but a stronger society may emerge in time. In the struggle to accept new immigrants of all persuasions and differences, America will have to address again and again its failure to come to terms with the African-American legacy. If it cannot come to terms with the legacy of slavery and racism, then America's decline will be irreversible; but I have some hope that America's irreversible heterogeneity in all areas of its social existence (including a redefinition of appropriate sex and gender distinctions) will lead, in time (but how much do we have?), to a redemption of our national sin (Franklin). These issues will require the attention of every academic and individual concerned with America, and I hope I have provided a diagnosis (X-ray), partial, to be sure, that will make possible some constructive criticism and research: blueprints for American studies.

When I started teaching overseas in 1983, a journey that has taken me to Turkey, Malaysia, Hong Kong, and South Africa, with academic tours of many other countries (India, Korea, Thailand, People's Republic of China, Philippines, and Taiwan), I thought I would be exporting useful American ideas and ideals. Little did I know that I would become "globalized" and "internationalized" in the process and that this redefinition of my own identity might serve as a guide for a re-examination of America in this and other studies. I left Amherst College in 1959, a year after my class (I had taken 1956–57 as a *Wanderjahr*, an augury of a life to come, I now see), with its motto in mind: *Terras Irradient* ("let us enlighten the world"); but it has turned out that the world has enlightened me, insofar as I can be enlightened.

The education of each generation turns out to be an exploration of that education itself, its generational imprint, its retrospective meaning. In the end, one's education becomes an item of history, a spot and frieze of time that allows one to comprehend one's moment in time. People have to go "somewhere else" to know "where they are." The process of discovery goes on, of course: of one's self, one's generation, one's country.

Re-vision

In revisiting this essay, I can see that I was more optimistic than I should have been about America's openness to new immigrants. The Bush administration's decision to build a fence along the Mexican border would seem to be a flagrant repudiation of our national history; but it's also true that the resistance to this barrier and the protests against it (with political implications that should favor the Democratic Party) are a reaffirmation of America's commitment to openness. The debate is not over. If anything, the crisis of "illegal immigration" has put the issue in the center of a national controversy about the relation of human rights (poverty, family structure) to the law. These issues will be contested in the presidential election of 2008 where more Hispanic-American candidates may be elected to office paradoxically than otherwise would have been the case.

Needless to say, the Iraq War forces every thoughtful America to question whether we learned anything as a nation about military interventions overseas after what many Americans would regard as the catastrophe of the Vietnam War. On the face of it, those neoconservative (neocon) ideologues who were able to convince President Bush in the aftermath of 9/11 that America needed to insist on its empiric power would seem to have carried the day.

But we must remember that this seemingly ill-fated use of force did come after the shock of 9/11 – an assault on America as repulsive to the general public as was Pearl Harbor.

It took the horror of Bin Laden's attack for Bush to overcome his self-announced resistance to "nation-building." Still, America is in Iraq. It has inflicted great numbers of casualties (over 30,000 by some estimates), and it has sustained heart-breaking losses of young men and women who, though often uninformed, are defending a word, "freedom," which they have been taught to value from birth.

In this sense, the Iraq War is not a violation of the essential principles I have enunciated in the original essay, but a misapplication, from my point of view, of those principles, a misapplication inconsistent with the historic values of the Anglo-American alliance. If studied and interpreted carefully in the decades to come, this war should encourage America to look for ways make the world a better place without destroying so much of it in the process. This war may teach us in the long run that there have to be better ways to ensure our survival, not as local and national species, but as a global habitat: a true habitat for humanity. History is long (America and Vietnam are now discussing military cooperation), and one should not lose hope in one's country's best possibilities because of any single costly error; but incidents and events such as Abu Ghraib, Haditha, and alleged "renditions" call into question the value of America's moral currency. This is a painful question for someone of my generation for whom the Nuremberg Trials set a worldwide standard for the defense of humanity.

If I had any concrete wish, at this point, it would be that when life in Iraq moves towards something like normalcy and a civil society, if it does, America will open its doors to new Iraqi immigrants who, like thousands who came from Vietnam after 1975, will add their traditions, cuisine, and voices to the uniqueness of America, as I see it, a One-world Nation. I would hope also that America's moral-military transgressions would lead to a reaffirmation of all binding international agreements and covenants such as the Geneva Convention.

Lady Liberty's torch may seem to be enshrouded in the fog of war, but I am enough of an American patriot to believe that the internationalism that is contained within this patriotism will insist, in the end, that the light won't go out. Once America renounces empiric ambitions, it can become a great nation among nations. Nothing induces national sanity so much as a measure of post-empiric humility, though dreams of former glory carry a potential danger with them as well.

CHAPTER FOUR

AN AMERICAN IN ANATOLIA

I 'm not quite sure when I first became aware of the Fulbright program. It seemed always to have been part of the educational and intellectual atmosphere for those who entered college in the 1950s and chose a career in higher education. But I do remember when it first affected my life directly: a young woman with whom I was in love – or certainly with whom I wanted to be in love (she embodied so many positive cultural and aesthetic values) – won a Fulbright just out of a small, progressive college, Sarah Lawrence, outside New York City, to study art history in Paris with one of the world's leading experts in what we now would call the Mediterranean Civilization.

I was dumbfounded. Here was someone, apparently like me, a contemporary, whose life would suddenly become different from mine (as it did) because she had won a Fulbright. I was proud and resentful at the same time: proud, of course, because someone so bright and resourceful, who had given her heart and songs (along with guitar playing) to me for a while, now had the added luster of being a Fulbright grantee; resentful because we would be separated and because I was not the recipient. I think I knew as well that she wouldn't come back into my life.

I was less worldly and sophisticated than my friend at that time, and I hadn't even made an application. But that didn't stop me from resenting her a little, and I made up my mind that one day I, too, would "go somewhere on a Fulbright," as I put it to myself, especially when I saw over the years what transformations had become possible for my friend – becoming fluent in French, singing and recording songs of Piaf and others. She even wrote a song about me, "Professor Wolf," which I heard her sing once in Paris. In time, when she became a writer, she even lived part of each year in Brittany.

These memories and associations haunted me through graduate school and my early years of teaching, and they became more compelling when, as the years passed, I became aware of colleagues, sometimes worthy and serious, sometimes gifted and brilliant, setting out for other parts of the world to accept Fulbright lectureships. Romance, achievement, and expansion were now conjoined in my mind as the meaning of the Fulbright.

But for many years, for various reasons, I didn't think of applying. Life and history's "cunning passages," as Eliot calls them, kept me toiling in the academic vineyards of Buffalo instead of teaching abroad, and, at a certain point, I became a single parent and had immense responsibilities to shoulder. Suddenly, I was a babysitter, chauffeur, tennis coach, and "laundress." I didn't have time to think about, much less apply for, a Fulbright.

But the time came when my daughter would leave home to go away to college. I had raised her, as my mother would have said, "to fly the coop," even though I knew I would deeply suffer the "empty nest" syndrome; I decided then that the right time had come. I, too, would leave home for a while. I would apply for a Fulbright and leave Buffalo, if I could, at the same time as my daughter. I knew that she might be able to come along with me if I were chosen, but I thought it best for us to make a clean break at first, if that would be possible.

I thought, at first, of applying for England and Israel. I had a love of English culture and literature, nurtured in the library of my somewhat British-style high school, Horace Mann in New York; moreover, as someone who mainly taught American literature, I was aware of the deep and complex literary and social relationships between the two countries over the centuries. We were in some way the seed of Albion. I also had written a graduate thesis on the American novelist, turned British citizen (some would say British writer), Henry James.

But as I thought about the possibility of teaching under the auspices of Fulbright, it seemed to me that cultural and literary difference was what the experience might offer to me and what I needed. I needed to put myself in a context where I could see my personal history and my country's in a somewhat different light. I wanted to see new modes of family relationships. I wanted to see how young people, different from my daughter and her friends, viewed the world, including the world of their parents. I wanted to replace the loss experience of letting go of a child with a more global perspective in which to view this loss and, finally, to redefine it. This kind of substitution, or restitution, has been one of the important legacies of my overseas teaching and world travel.

At the same time, I was intrigued by the possibility of going to an ancient homeland. It seemed to me that Israel would provide key terms of difference, even as it would allow me the opportunity to share my miniature experience of recent dispossession with people who also knew loss, many of whom had lost everything.

Because of the needs of Fulbright for that year, however, I was given the opportunity instead to go to Turkey. I was stunned at first. I knew so little about Turkey: remnants of elementary and high school learning, fragments of media images, Hollywood movies set in harems with flimsy robes. My appointment seemed remote from the associations that clung to the young woman who had set off for Paris a quarter of a century before.

But I sensed, even in the midst of my apprehension, that my state of cultural innocence might turn out for the best. I would be tested and I might discover – as I did – that initially remote and apparently inhospitable places could become warm and homelike. I sensed that my loss might become or lead me toward and make me ready for a global gain. Still I was unprepared when I accepted an appointment as a Fulbright lecturer in American literature for 1983-1984 to Ankara University.

I didn't even know that Ankara had become the capital after the revolution of 1923. I had assumed that Istanbul was the seat of government. I even may have thought that there were two cities – Istanbul and Constantinople – on the Bosporus. I didn't know that the Bosporus, connecting the Black and Marmora Seas, divided Turkey into two land masses – one small, lying to the west: Thrace; the other, larger, to the east: Anatolia. I didn't know that this meeting place of West and East at the confluence of the Golden Horn, Bosporus, and Marmora Sea represented one of the crucibles and crossroads of global history.

I didn't know that Turkey was a Moslem country that looked, by and large, to the West, rather than to Islam, for its cultural identity; that Ataturk ("father of the Turks") was a figure as revered among schoolchildren as George Washington; or that the hands on the ornate clocks in Dolmabahce Palace (the last palace of the Ottoman sultans and Ataturk's residence in Istanbul) would stay fixed at the moment of his death in 1938. I didn't know that Ataturk, virtually single-handedly, had banned the fez, torn off the veil, substituted the Latin alphabet for Arabic, and catapulted Turkey into the modern world after driving the Greeks into the sea at Smyrna (now Izmir).

I had trace memories about the Young Turks, and I had heard of "Turkish delight," but probably assumed it was a close encounter of an erotic nature. So I was ignorant and in some sense open to new arrangements of time and space, history, and geography. With a received faith in the "broadening values" of travel and beneficial effects of "difference," with few preconceptions, many apprehensions, too much luggage and less anxiety, I left Buffalo in September 1983.

I discovered in Paris, racing to make the connection for Istanbul, that the Turkish Airlines counter had been blown up by Armenian "terrorists" a month before and that it was now moved every day. "Where is it today?" I asked. "Who knows? You'll have to look," was the Gallic agent's logical response. I mention this part of the antic journey only to hint at a parable about travel, self-discovery, and education: You don't always find what you're looking for directly, and you sometimes find what you're not expecting with simplicity, vividness, and sudden, heartbreaking tenderness. You never know where and when you will see life and yourself somewhat differently.

I soon discovered that Turkey was part of the same ancient Aegean world that had nurtured the now better-known Classical Greeks (a sore point for contemporary Turks). Troy and Ephesus, to name two of a hundred major sites, lay on Turkish soil; Herodotus was born in Bodrum (then Halicarnassus), an Aegean coastal resort now called "Bedroom" by the Turkish jet-setters and disco set.

Turkey was so old that Turkish invaders had sacked its Byzantine capital, Constantinople, in 1453, half a century before the discovery of America by European voyagers. This was old, older than my Russian grandfather, so I prepared myself imaginatively for teaching in a hoary university like Oxford or Coimbra in Portugal.

I wondered if I would teach in a robe, perhaps one with feathers or fur, and stroll across tiled courtyards with young scholars who would, glancing at gilt-edged illuminated books, ask wise questions. I was looking, after all, for tradition, civilization, a sense of accrued time, memorable place.

I learned on my first day in the Faculty of Language, History, and Geography, *Dil Tarih Cografya* (our Arts and Letters, more or less), that my faculty had been organized and built in the 1930s. I was as old as the faculty. When I told a colleague that my undergraduate alma mater had been founded in 1821 and that I had earned another degree from a university, Columbia University, then King's College, established in 1754, he asked, "What is it like to go to venerable institutions?" I was speechless; I had come after all as a representative of the New World, looking for antique ways, Byzantine design, and glimpses of Attic Aegean architecture.

I felt this doubleness throughout my teaching experience in Turkey. I represented an older society, with respect to the organization of higher education, the checks and balances of liberal democracy, and the application of science and technology to everyday living. Colleagues would often say, if I were critical of static bureaucracy, imperious treatment of students, obsolete caliphatic patterns of hierarchy separating junior from senior faculty, "Give us time; you've been doing this kind of thing longer than we have."

Everyone assumed, nonetheless, that I expected to have the latest state-of-the-art technologies as an aid to teaching: video and audiotapes, electric typewriter, Xerox machine, personal computer, etc. Students, always self-effacing in Turkey, apologized for the lack of heat in the building, poor lighting, scored blackboards, soot-filled air that wafted in from the railroad tracks outside our classroom window. "Soon we'll have your means of pollution control," they would say, knowing that the military government wanted F-14s, not a higher quality of expensive fuel for its people.

America was somehow old and new. America was far away, farther than 99 percent of my students would ever be able to afford to visit, but it was there as an image, an omnipresent visual fact of life through the export of television and movies (even if they were grade-B reruns), cars (even if they were 1958 Chevrolets), and song (even if it was Nat King Cole). Sometimes I felt as if I were reliving America in the fifties. American entertainment gave Turkey a second environment. Russia, though it shares a border, was invisible to all except the USAF logistical analysts.

I represented older traditions of secular learning to my students, even as they subscribed to the sacred laws of Islam; they wanted to know about the Empire State Building (the "late" World Trade Center had not captured the near Third World's imagination yet, perhaps because it lacked a spire), space shuttle launches, and moon landings – the most dazzling proof to the Turks of American technological supremacy. Nothing pleased my students more than when I arranged for them to see a film in the temperature-controlled and comfortable screening rooms of the then United States Information Service (USIS) building. They couldn't believe that the cultural officers welcomed us!

I was in the paradoxical and somewhat topsy-turvy position of teaching them a literature, ours, that pre-dated their own modern state (1923) – the Puritans, Poe, Hawthorne, Whitman, Emerson – although I represented a window to modernity. I had come to teach the new and discover the old, but I was beginning to discover the old in my own culture and the problem of the new, so to speak, for my students.

I also was beginning to see more clearly the price my culture had paid for modernity as I traveled through their time-worn villages, and I had mixed feelings about what it would mean for my students and their country to try to catch up with us. The act of talking about books was not so simple. I approached American books from a point of view fixed in a time and place different from theirs. How would we meet?

Literary interpretation and discussion became something more than identifying myself with one school of criticism or another as I taught in Ankara second-, third-, and fourth-year classes in one room, alongside the railroad track, watching cheap, sulfurous coal being freighted in from the provinces. I struggled all year to find ways in which we could understand how and why Turks looked at the world in terms somewhat different from me, their American teacher, and I could never forget that I was a representative of my country, for better and worse.

My gestures, my dress, to say nothing of my language and what I said were, to dress up the issue a little, a semiotic system. If I wore an overcoat in class, as I did once or twice, to protest quietly the lack of heat (all that coal was rolling somewhere other than to our university), I was making a statement as important as anything I might say about our books, for their professors would not – in those still politically anxious times, in the aftermath of near civil war – have acted so brazenly. Books were important, yes, and so was what I wore when I talked about those books.

And these books were precious. They were dearly bought new and equally valuable in a usable secondhand state. Many of my students came from rural families with incomes of less than two thousand dollars a year. One student from the Black Sea region, "Zecki," gave me a kilo of hazelnuts as a lavish expression of his father's appreciation for my role as teacher ("hodja"). My students were concerned, in talking about books, as they were concerned in buying them, with what was basic, essential, necessary, and useful. Many of them moved on to lead more affluent lives. Zecki became a diplomat, posted to Israel, and is now an industrialist in Albania. A poor, but brilliant, young woman, with whom I had a decorous but private liaison, joined the Ministry of Culture and is now an expert in EU projects.

They could understand Steinbeck more easily than Poe because the labor of farming was a more obvious feature of their national lives than nightmare; Twain made more sense than Washington Irving's fable, "Rip Van Winkle," because illiteracy was a more common condition than playing nine-pins with leprechauns; they preferred *The Scarlet Letter* to Emerson's essay "Self-Reliance" because Turkish family and social life were still scrupulously traditional and conservative: A young couple did not date until a marriage arrangement had been made, and premarital sex can lead to a woman's banishment from her family or, worse, can drive her to the Bunuel-like Alley of the Lonely in Istanbul.

They preferred Hemingway to Faulkner because he was easier to read, and they needed to learn functional English if they wanted careers in the government, the military, tourism, or business. Money talks in Turkey for a struggling generation, and it speaks English. They preferred Thornton Wilder's *Our Town* to his *The Skin of Our Teeth* because one affirmed social cohesion, continuity between generations, stability of village life, the need for companionship and friendship, while the other inverted time and space, showed a world absurdly out of joint. Turks do not understand aloneness, loneliness, or social pathology. They gather ritualistically in groups – in homes, barbershops, tailor shops, offices – to drink tea (cay, pronounced "chai"), the elixir of social life.

My students were, in a word, essentially premodern. Hawthorne was, in a sense, their contemporary. I had come bearing news of the new, and my students had unearthed the Puritan tradition in our literature. I had come looking for civilization, expecting Byzantine ornateness, exotic architecture, and exquisite figures in the carpet and found, instead, a culture largely made up of 40,000 villages, with a dignity based on "poor" values: the lean, bare, and economical. The modern temper, to say nothing of the abstruseness of Postmodernism, made little sense to them.

There is, of course, a Turkish avant-garde, but its influence doesn't go much beyond Istanbul, and even there it doesn't spring from or touch the life of the people. Postmodernist attitudes are the privilege, or affectation, of a small class of Turks who have been educated in America, Germany, Britain, France, and Italy (in about that order). Nearly two million Turks live in Germany as industrial workers ("Gastarbeiter"), not students of advanced aesthetic culture.

Literary study in English of American literature meant something more practical and, potentially, more dangerous for my students in Turkey than it did at home. Knowing and speaking English opened doors for students in banking, tourism, and the foreign ministry, to say nothing of teaching and study abroad. At the same time, embracing certain American ideas of individualism, set deeply in our literature from the Quaker John Woolman through Emerson to Robert Frost and the Beat writers, might inaugurate a path of inquiry that would lead to difficult and risky political choices.

An editor of one journal told me she did not know one literary person possessing honor and courage who had not been arrested at one time or another under the alternate regimes of Right and Left that have shaped Turkey's domestic political history since the death of Ataturk. I submitted an essay to this editor and referred in it – historically, not from a partisan point of view – to the Paris communes of the early 1870s. The editor encouraged me to delete the reference for both our sakes.

I was, in this sense, sometimes wary of teaching certain texts, such as Thoreau's "Civil Disobedience," as if I might encourage too facile a sense of opposition to established authority. Many of my students would return to provincial communities, not to the salons of Istanbul. I could not encourage easy assumptions about the dismantling of authority. I had to know where I was. I was teaching the young in Ankara, not Berkeley.

I began to see contrastively into the displacement of tradition in America, the substitution of media families for real families, the replication of experience through symbols, slogans, and soap operas. I wondered how my students could bring about necessary social and political change while maintaining a dignified stability rooted in the rhythms of agrarian and sacred life, and I didn't know how they were going to become new (and I, old) without a painful rearrangement of the self in relation to place and history.

I didn't know the answers and took some comfort in riding the archaic (1920s) night train – the Istanbul Express – on the first step of my return to the U.S.; I rocked and swayed in a middle region of time between cultures and wondered how much the leaders of my country paid attention to the subtle ratios of difference in time and geography between countries in making decisions that shape the future of the world.

It seemed to me, as I was about to leave Turkey (and that awareness has grown since then), that foreign policy often misses the actual life of the people about whom we, as a government, are making policy. I hoped, as I was about to leave Turkey, that some of the U.S. graduate students whom I met in Turkey as Fulbrighters would enter the Foreign Service eventually as diplomats or cultural officers. Those American students who had rubbed shoulders with Turkish students would have a clearer sense of the needs and style of the country than people trained strictly within theoretical frameworks and the terms of power. And who knows what difference these people would make in the next forty years?

I thought of these corridors of time and, crossing the "Bos" at dawn, with the sun slanting across the missile-like minarets on the European side, wondered what sense I would make in the future of the drum-beats and flutes I had heard at a village wedding on the edge of the Aegean, while hillside fields were burned, preparing the earth for harvest.

What would I make of the child who had kissed my hand and touched it reverentially to her forehead? How would I relate these gestures to the New World? I wasn't sure, but for a moment, as Europe and Asia were joined in the morning flood of light across the Bosporus Bridge, I felt suspended in time. Turkey is like that, sometimes, especially on a spring night in the Passage of Flowers.

I have been back for more than two decades, though I have returned briefly twice. I don't think of Turkey every day, or even every week, and I can't say that an outsider would think that I had changed very much. I probably haven't, but there are moments, in the classroom, especially when I look at a foreign student (Remla, Unal, Jaehwan), or when I talk with a visiting Fulbright scholar (Biyot, Adi, Mihali), when I am painfully aware of the adventure and excitement, the displacement and even fear, of being a cultural outsider.

I think of myself in Turkey, of my friend in Paris all those years ago. I try to imagine my Turkish students in the U.S.; I think of my daughter making a long and strange trip to visit me in Turkey (leaving the U.S. for the first time, coming through Germany, losing a day for the first time). I imagine us all as strangers on the globe and try, imperceptibly I suppose, to think of us as a community of people who can empathize with each other's separation and, sometimes, isolation. Privileged exiles, if you will, we feel closer to one another, even at a distance. This is one of the major themes and lessons of these travel essays. And when spring comes to Buffalo, as it usually does, my heart goes back to the "Bos."

Re-vision

Turkey opened the door to the greater world for me, and I remain grateful to it. Although I was not an American who assumed that America was "the best damn country in the world," I had been raised at a time when it had been easy to think of America as a privileged and successful country. We had escaped the ravages of war on the home front, and most of Europe had welcomed us as liberators. Our great ally, Britain, had not been so fortunate. Had I not gone to Turkey, I might not have learned that there is cultural diversity as well as bio-diversity; and if one is to discover all of one's potentialities and to flourish as a whole person, then he needs to explore the variety of global systems.

I learned in Turkey that I had been denied certain forms of familial and social cohesion that spoke to deep needs in my personality as an individual, teacher, and writer. As the reign of Suleiman the Magnificent (1520-1566) had given asylum to victims of the Spanish Inquisition, so Turkey had welcomed me and given me a deeper sense of what "home" can mean. I forgot this gift for a while, but the "poor young woman" and I have found each other again at a point in our lives where each understands the implications of aloneness and loneliness; and v⋔ it looks as if we shall together make a "symbolic community" more substantial.

Somewhat imprisoned in her Turkish family, she can grow in a relationship with an American companion who will encourage her independence; I, who have lived the life of a somewhat fragmented family man, can take comfort in the value she assigns to companionship. Our reunion defines some of the value and significance of international relations at an intimate and social level. That she is a secular Turkish Moslem and I am a secular American Jew makes this reunion all the more significant at a time when the alleged clash of civilizations seems to be tearing the world apart.

Turkey has changed, though it is still an "illiberal democracy" (a former student writes) as the trial of Orhan Pamuk demonstrated, but it is knocking on the door of the EU, and will have to grant greater freedom to its citizens (especially the Kurds) and intellectuals if it wishes to be admitted. Still it remains a traditional society in many ways. My marriage foundered in the creative chaos of the American 1960s. I can't turn back the clock, but I can buy a new watch.

One of the lessons that has emerged through my travels has been the paradox that much of the world needs certain of our freedoms more urgently than we do, even as we would profit more from some imported traditions. The world needs a merger of cultures more than it does a clash of civilizations. This is likely to happen in the short run only at the level of individuals, but it is a start. When Gentile Bellini went to the Ottoman capital (1479-80) at the invitation of Sultan Medmed II to paint the court, he brought his Venetian genius with him; he returned with the impress of the Islamic world on his work.

CHAPTER FIVE

THE LAST DAYS OF CHUA X: WOMEN, WORK, AND THE LATE COLONIAL TROPICS

One of the first words you learn in Malaysia, and I suppose this is true of comparable words in other Southeast Asian countries, is "amah" (Chinese "nurse" or "maid," Tamil "mother"). You learn it in the lobby of the hotel where you are staying, as I learned it in the P.J. (Petaling Jaya, "Happy Wood") Hilton (initials are fashionable and common in Malaysia – doubtless an imitation of British Oxbridge nomenclature). It seems to come with gin and tonic as you wait for your real estate agent to find the "right bungalow" for you.

I did not have much of a chance to think about whether I wanted a housekeeper. My real estate agent informed me that a housekeeper was available if I "wanted one." It seemed reasonable to give her a try, and besides, it was clear that everyone else in our group of American teachers was going to have some "help," and I didn't want to stand out at that point of arrival when belonging to some group is important. Having an amah was part of the social system. To the Brits it meant social standing; to the Americans it meant an upgraded style of suburban living – an outreach of conspicuous consumption.

I assumed she would be Chinese Malaysian, because the agent was, and I understood at once that each of the three races in Malaysia (Chinese, Indian, and Malay) looked after itself if possible. This pleased me. I was a native New Yorker and had spent a lot of my childhood eating Chinese food with my parents on Sunday in the House of Chan on Broadway. It was something like a Sabbath. I may even have thought I was Chinese at an early age, just as I later wondered if I might be part Iroquois when I was sent off to a summer camp with a name like Spread Eagle.

Chua was part of the system and she came with the house – she was an attractive feature like the air-con, the overhead fans, the marble floors, the teak woodwork, the television, and the garden. Despite the attractive terms of our employment, we all felt we were entitled to gracious living because we had been willing to give up the comforts of home. It did not take long to see that life in the tropics, if you had some hard currency to spare, was actually a realization of the longed-for luxuries of home (usually the promises that TV makes) and that many expats would be reluctant to give up the "hardships" of overseas work. So arrangements were made, and I waited for Chua to come on a Saturday afternoon.

She arrived by taxi during a downpour and lightning storm, virtually concealed by a large umbrella as she stepped out of the cab, arms full of various bags. She clearly intended to stay for a while. As I let her through the iron gates into the house, she stepped out of her sandals, as one must do in Malaysia, put down her sacks, and handed me a packet of letters.

"Read," she said.

She disappeared into what she knew was the maid's room as I glanced at her character references. They were all very positive, attesting to her incredible loyalty and hard work, though they also suggested, without being specific, that she could be stubborn and a little "bullish" about wanting praise and good letters of recommendation for future employment. It seemed that she was now working for a German diplomat five and a half days a week and wanted to work for me the other day and a half. Her need and goal were, apparently, to work all the time.

She appeared in the living room in her white uniform, standing regimentally stiff.

"Like?" she asked.

I wasn't sure if she meant the dress or the letters, but I said, yes.

"Good, work now."

I was a little disappointed that she spoke so little English. I knew we would be condemned to primitive Tarzan-like conversations and that I would be accused of stereotyping if I ever wanted to write about her (such things occur to writers). I was also a little disappointed that she was not a Dragon Lady beauty. She was small, but stocky, with an American football player's legs, and she had half-closed eyes when she didn't wear her glasses, which she rarely did. She seemed determined to go blind. I sometimes thought that she wanted to get her life of labor over with as quickly as possible, or that she was trying to punish the system in some irrational way.

I had hoped, foolishly, in those first weeks in the tropics, when you recall all the exotic and erotic tales that you have ever read, that my housekeeper would be a "native" beauty, but I knew I had been saved from my worst American male fantasies and indecencies when Chua showed up. I knew it was best for me, as a visiting teacher and bachelor, to behave with a measure of respect, even in the tropics of one's Gauguin-like imagination.

But I wondered if it would be wise to have Chua stay over. Could I trust myself during lonely nights? (I didn't doubt, given my Colonial preconceptions, that I could "have her" if I so wished.) And what would happen if and when I did get involved with someone? And suppose that person wasn't Chinese? Would there be racial and religious conflicts?

I decided to go shopping while I thought these things over. I went to the "Jaya" supermarket by "call taxi," as I went everywhere by taxi during my year in Kuala Lumpur. It's an inexpensive means of travel for foreigners, especially

Westerners, and it eliminates many problems – such as driving on the left (one of the many traces of British Malaya), or losing your car during a monsoon flood.

But using call taxis as I did also brought upon one a sense of Colonial omnipotence and power. It gave me the feeling that I could enact my will at a moment's notice. It wasn't unlike other aspects of living as an expat on overseas pay in a country that, though wonderfully livable in many respects, had not yet attained the status of an NIC (newly industrialized country).

When I returned from the market, Chua was there to greet me at the gate. Her "servant" clock knew how long it would take a "bachelor boss," I suppose, to do the shopping. I had no sooner come in with the shopping bags than they were taken from my hands, effortlessly, it seemed. Needless to say, I didn't have to tell Chua where to put things, and before long afternoon tea appeared and after that, with some gestural indications of preference on my part, dinner.

No sooner was dinner over than Chua began to do the wash, scrub the marble floors, mend some clothing, water the plants, and iron all the clothing she had washed – including socks and anything that could be laid flat on a table. It was clear that she wouldn't finish her chores, mainly self-imposed, until well after midnight, and I knew that I wouldn't ask her to leave at that time to go "home," wherever and whatever home was.

It took me a month to find out that she had a room in the German diplomat's house. I assumed that it was a cramped space for a thirty-something-year-old woman (as close a determination as I can make about Chua's age), for though she looked about fifty, I knew from the references that she had been working about twenty years, and it was clear that she had labored from middle adolescence and worked all her life, that she had known little other than work.

I was pleased to learn that she was living with the diplomat. I had seen a wide range of possible housing in Kuala

Lumpur, including, of course, the conspicuous squatters' huts along the Klang River, where lobsters once crawled from the Straits of Malacca and where now a hundred years of tin silt has turned the banks and water into a gray-brown sludge.

Chua stayed that night and every Saturday night for the year that I was in Malaysia. She worked all the time as she had worked the first day. She never rested, sometimes slept on the floor of the study, where there was air-con, if her room became too hot, and she got up at first light to resume her duties. I would try to get her to stop sometimes, and she would occasionally, and we learned to talk a bit to one another; but essentially she lived to work, if I may put it this way, as much as she worked to live.

She wanted three things from me: fair payment, a glowing letter of reference at the end, and for me to help her get a job with another Westerner when I left, for she knew what it meant to work for a Malaysian family within the terms of their economy and their indifference to the lives and fates of housekeepers like Chua.

She wanted these things from me, and she always made sure to remind me of them whenever she did something kind or considerate. It was impossible for me to separate her soul or personality from her need to work so that she might visit her mother twice a year (for the Chinese New Year with a money gift and on her mother's birthday) and have some money saved for her later years. This was a particularly pressing need, because a lover had stolen all the savings of ten years' previous work a year before she had begun to work for the diplomat and me.

She had seen me get very upset one evening when I learned that a trusted friend in America had betrayed me over a money matter and put me in a difficult situation. I had cried over this – one of the few times I had shed tears in my adult life. To comfort me, I suppose, to show that she understood the "boss" and was loyal to him, she managed to tell me her "story," as she put it.

"I have same story, boss," she kept saying, and I managed to pry the details from her: the usual stuff of universal disappointment – a lover, a loan, a disappearance. I learned further, when she showed me her purse and her documents, that she kept all her money with her. I wrote out a note for her to give to the diplomat, instructing him to open a bank account for her. I felt good about this and still do. Since I probably couldn't give her something valuable of an immaterial nature, I wanted her at least to have something concrete.

I never knew whether Chua acted out of compassionate or self-interested motives, for her livelihood depended upon my good will and good health. After she had worked for me for about a month, I developed an enigmatic pain in my left leg that was diagnosed finally as pain referred from a strained lower back. I was told to lie still for as long as possible with my legs propped on a pillow.

When Chua saw me lying in this prostrate position, she must have assumed that I wasn't long for this world. In her work culture, people, especially women, only lie down for such an extended period of time when they are dying or giving birth, and, though I was an American, it was unlikely that I was giving birth. She brought me a strange black unguent to rub on my leg. When I rejected it, she assured me that she would sleep outside my bedroom door to keep evil spirits away. It was too difficult to explain that evil spirits, at least of the lower back kind, probably weren't my problem.

In the evening, she burned a sacred joss stick on my behalf. I knew that she would do everything possible to keep her boss alive, and I was grateful for her ministrations. It was easy to believe – half-way around the world, with no one else to look after me – that she cared about me as I cared about her, but I couldn't be sure then or now.

I decided to give myself a birthday party. Birthdays are harder to get through alone when you're overseas than when you're alone at home. Chua was an experienced hand at giving Western-style birthday parties, not that a Chinese Malaysian party would have been all that different. Major Western holidays have worked themselves deep into the mind and soul of commercial Asia and are part of the mall and hotel culture of the economic Tigers and those who "wannabe" Tigers. These holidays are part of the popular culture and take their place with Michael Jackson videos and David Copperfield spectacles. I saw more made of Easter in the lobby of the Pan Pacific Hotel and the outsize atrium of THE MALL than I have ever seen anywhere in the United States.

Among other things, Chua sent me a card. On the outside it says, "For a wonderful Boss." On the inside it says, "With many thanks for being so nice to work for, with many wishes for a very happy birthday." I was touched by this card. Chua could have had a meal out, given her diet (bread and soup; she complained of stomach pains with other food), for the price of the card.

But I couldn't get away from the fact that she was reinforcing our social-economic arrangement. I do not know what other kind of card she could have sent me, for, among other things, she would not have thought it possible to send any other kind of card. She would not have thought about the selection of a card as a problem at all. She did what was "natural." That is, she did exactly what the Colonial "situation" called for.

I am tempted to say that Chua's insecurities were endless in this way, though I don't think that "insecurity" is the right word. I would say that her uncertainty about survival was boundless. She was being clear-headed, not anxious, with its neurotic connotations, about the riskiness of her position. Once she lost her connection with the Western-European employment world, her life would take a sudden and possibly desperate downward turn.

When Christmas came, Chua sent me, of course, another work-related card: "It's nice to wish a boss like you a Merry Christmas Day." If I had planned to spend the rest of my life in the tropics, I would have taught her, somehow, to send me a Chanukah card; but I'm not sure that a lifetime would have been long enough for that instruction, or "tuition," as they say in outposts of the Raj and Empire. I had failed after months of effort to explain to her how it was possible for a non-Moslem also not to want to eat pork.

And so it went, and so it goes. I recently got a letter from the German diplomat and his wife, assuring me that they would try to help Chua get a job with a European or American when they left. I had urged them strongly to help her in this way. With their letter is included a note from Chua in which she says, among other things: "I hope come K.L." I believe she is referring to my possible return to Kuala Lumpur. And she says, referring to last year, "I would like to thank you for the New Year money a $100 which is equal to M$268.30." I assume the diplomats helped her with this sentence, if not the calculation. She concludes by saying that "I still do not have a part-time job."

She includes with the letter her full name and home address: Chua Lai Choo, city of Ipoh, State of Perak. It is only now that I think of her having a full name, of having the potentiality of full personhood, as we might say, of her inhabiting her name, as I like to think that I possess mine.

When I left Malaysia, I gave Chua Lai Choo all the household goods that I didn't want to send back to America. I gave them as an expression of my gratitude for her loyal service and because I worried about her future, her later years. What would happen if she got displaced from the system or lost her eyesight? She would doubtless return to Ipoh and live with one of her relatives, but it would be a source of embarrassment to her if she returned without enough money saved to live out the rest of her days and if she returned without sufficient household goods to sustain the family's honorable name.

Chua made it clear that she would hold these possessions for me until I returned to Malaysia. She did not want to believe that her "good boss," as she came to call me, would leave her to fend for herself among all the other 'amahs' of Kuala Lumpur.

I hope to return to Kuala Lumpur one day and to find out how Chua is getting along. If she is in Ipoh, I will go there and visit her. I imagine us sitting in the living room of her Kampong chalet with a soft jungle breeze coming in through the atap, palm-leaf, and bamboo weave of the raised building. The house will look familiar, especially the kitchen, where I hope to see my teapot and dishes.

I imagine that a neighbor or two will look in to see the special visitor who has come to see one of the "richest" ladies in the "kampong" (village). If she can, I'm sure she will serve me tea – free of charge this time because I will be a guest, not her boss. If she is feeble and if her sight has failed, I will serve her. If she feels old enough, she will let me do this because she is Chinese, though Malaysian Chinese to be sure.

But I'm not confident that I will return to confirm these speculations. I'll probably just send money as a gift each year for the Chinese New Year, wrapped appropriately in dragon-red paper, and address it to Chua Lai Choo, boss one day, I hope, of her own house, though even this impulse may be a tropical fancy, the play of the wind in the heart of a reluctant, but enchanted, American traveler.

Re-vision

Chua stopped sending birthday cards after a few years, and I haven't seen nor heard from her again.

As much as overseas living made it possible for me to imagine that I was living in a social world with deep registers of feeling and mutual understanding as a consequence of "displaced" people – expats, travelers, overseas workers – coming together with urgent needs for connection, it also made clear, in the passage of time, that these connections can be fragile and fleeting.

Except for a small community of people with whom one was able to keep up in various ways, it became clear to me that these friendships, liaisons, associations, and sudden affinities could best be preserved in writing, as sad and guilty as one might feel about, in effect, abandoning certain people who had helped one to live away from home.

One could revisit the past in literary terms and try to give it a form and significance that may not have been apparent in the original experience. I gave a title to a collection of travel letters in 1992 that gets at what I am trying to say here: *A Version of Home: Letters from the World*. One could pay homage in literary terms to those people who had helped one live away from home.

I left home to find a deeper sense of home and then had to move on if I wanted to see something like the whole world (an impulse that had roots in a narrow and provincial childhood, even though it was a New York City childhood). For different reasons, I walked away from many intimate and satisfying relationships. I could preserve them only by losing them and then writing about them. The losses took the register of the bonds. I left my heart at many bus and railroad stations and airports, but I learned something about the heart, mine for starters.

If a reader asked why I had to leave America to find a deeper sense of home, I would have to write at length about "loneliness" as a cultural attribute of the somewhat New World. If all French novels deal with adultery and all British novels touch on class relations, American culture puts loneliness and identity (and the relationship between them) at the center of its preoccupations.

This may be true especially of the academic world where colleagues tend to live in bubbles of their own blowing. Milan Kundera uses the word "graphomania" in his *The Book of Laughter and Forgetting* to describe these kinds of enclosures. He is speaking of the way in which each writer-intellectual thinks that his created world is the only world and is threatened by the existence of other alleged worlds. His Swiftian view of flying islands of thought turn out to be all too true and contemporary. I address this theme in several of the essays in this collection.

CHAPTER SIX

A PASSENGER TO INDIA:
ON TRAVEL AND WRITING

I knew that I would go to India from the time that a
chef in a now-long-defunct Far Rockaway hotel read
my palm and told me that I had a lifeline that would carry
me around the world. I couldn't figure out how this undeniably
sage figure had ended up in the kitchen of my father's broken-
down summer resort, but he seemed to be the genuine article.

He resembled in every observable way the imperturbable
and mystic figures who appeared in the swashbuckling and
exotic movies of the post–World War II era, and, if I had any
doubts about his authenticity, they were soon dispelled by the
works of Somerset Maugham, especially *The Razor's Edge*.

There was no doubt in my mind that one day I would go
"somewheres East of Suez where the best is like the worst,"
words that were sung incessantly in Wednesday morning
assembly in my high school to prepare us for a worldly life.
The road to "Mandalay" (1890) seemed to be the most
important route in the world. I assumed I would cross the Bay
of Bengal one day. It was just a matter of time.

As it turned out, I had more than thirty years to prepare
myself, because it wasn't until I went to teach in Malaysia in
1988 that I had a chance to cross the Bay of Bengal. I had been

promising an Indian friend for years that I would visit him, and I knew that I wouldn't be able to let him down once I was on the edge of the Pacific Rim.

I had thirty years to prepare myself to receive the great impression that India would inevitably make. I read the Upanishadic literature in high school; I paid particular attention to the Hindu references in Thoreau's *Walden* and tried to understand Emerson's interest in the Brahmins. I saw each part of Satyajit Ray's *The Apu Trilogy* as it came out. I was enchanted by Jean Renoir's *The River* (1951). I read Gandhi's *The Story of My Experiment with Truth* and George Orwell's "Reflections on Gandhi."

I became friendly with Indian students, writers, and scholars as we crossed paths along our mutual literary and academic journeys, and I carried on a frank and sustained correspondence with two Indian friends for more than a decade. I learned in these exchanges that my Indian friends, for all their flights of imagination and myth, could be more specific about the facts of their lives – both social and biological – than I ever would have dared to be. Although I hadn't been there, I felt that I knew India, its soul, its mind; it was just a matter of time before I discovered the actual embodiment of a spiritual home. If I delayed making my trip to India, it might have been as a result of the expectation and fear that I would discover that India was, or could become, more of a home than America to me. I may have feared that India would challenge decades of striving on my part, decades of self and professional definition in which American and Western notions of, and preoccupations with, the Ego (as we called it in the Fifties and Sixties) or Self (as we have been calling it in the Seventies and Eighties) were dominant.

India represented, I realized as I began to pack my bag for the flight from Kuala Lampur to Singapore (whence I would fly to Calcutta), the apparent negation of so much that I, many of my colleagues, and the academic profession stood for in America. India might go against the advancement of Self through writing and the promotion of that writing.

If India didn't represent the negation of the ends of this project (the advancement of learning), it certainly seemed at the outset to represent a denial at least of the means of making a career in the American academy of letters: India might go against the essentially noncooperative and isolated commitments of time and energy to the production of works to advance one's name and standing that defines, to a large extent, the transatlantic academy.

And there was the possibility that a trip to India would force me to revise my understanding of writing itself, my sense of language and what it might accomplish, in its description and correction of the world. To go to India, to take its impression, might be to undo my relations to academia and culture. In another way, the trip to India, which carried the expectation of a "passage," might draw out of me feelings about writing that would be as discomfiting as the preconceptions that it might override. India might make so much of a case for experience, might be so much of an experience, that language itself would be challenged.

India might force me to become, or try to become, an "outdoors" critic and writer, a critic and writer whose every thought and idea, whose every theory, if I were bold enough to have one, would have to be tested against the actualities of experiences, actualities so overwhelming as to move them beyond the status of mere facts. The facts of India might make the "indoor" preoccupations of a writer and filmmaker, such as Alain Robbe-Grillet, seem gratuitous and trivial. In discussing his film *La Belle Captive*, Robbe-Grillet took pride in the fact that his film was made almost entirely within the confines of one house whose interior was redesigned for different scenes and whose spatial confines also were used to create illusions of outdoor shots, as well (especially the dreamy motorcycle scenes). He rests easy with "virtual reality." I thought of my trip to India as I watched this movie and thought how difficult it is in that "wounded" land to move indoors to protect oneself – in fact or theory or in fantasy – from the incursions of suffering humanity.

If you travel by train in India, as you are likely to do as a matter of necessity and economy, you become aware of your body and the bodies of others. In anything less than "air-con" first class, and even there, the toilets are likely to be stuck and stuffed, so that you meditate on your bowels most of the time; and if you arrive at a station in the early morning, your image of arrival – the image of India you are likely to remember – is of a squatting man, sarong clutched up over his knees, trying to relieve himself safely out of the bush.

If you make eye contact with him, he will look at you with that studied indifference that exposed people cultivate to deal with the embarrassments of public living that poverty and underdevelopment make unavoidable. And when you pull into a station, past the bundled and shrouded bodies of waiting (possibly dead) passengers and displaced villagers, imploring hands will press through the bars of the window; and, if you give a few rupees, as you are likely to do if you're American, you will touch the hand of India and you will wonder, despite your compassion and humanitarianism, if you have become untouchable.

So, even though India makes it difficult to think of oneself as an "indoor" writer, the same facts of life, in their overwhelming nakedness, push you back, make you want to retreat into a safe enclave, some colonial enclosure, some touristic haven (New Kenilworth), some Anglo-Indian club (Nizam) where gin and tonic flows freely and where the "natives" (no longer dirt-covered hands) wear turbans. Even as India (at least the parts of it that I saw – West Bengal, the Gangetic plain, Orissa, and Andhra Pradesh) makes it difficult, if not impossible, to shrink from facts, to deny actualities; even as India makes one reaffirm the Orwellian imperative to face "the surface of the earth," to confront "solid objects," so India drives one away, forces one to seek shelter, from those facts as an act of self-preservation.

Nothing prepares one for India, at least for Calcutta, at an emotional level. Three decades does not prepare the privileged American or Westerner for what he is likely to encounter as he drives (or is driven) from the airport to the heart of Calcutta. One may have spent these decades preparing oneself for a passage from self-consciousness to the transcendent and trans-personal mythologies of India; one even may have practiced something like Hindu patience itself in getting ready to meet the incarnations of the gods and goddesses, the reigning deities, whose images are impressed on every outstanding concavity and convexity of banyan tree and cave in India; but, on arrival, one is likely to shudder and shrink in the backseat of a broken-down Ambassador taxi and face the fact that one is likely to be a "passenger" in India, an intellectual tourist; that one is more likely to watch and recoil against what one sees than to participate in the daily rituals of living and dying that mark the city streets as clearly as signs and billboards do in the United States.

At least this is how I felt when I landed in Calcutta and slid into the backseat of a musty sedan that the U.S.I.S. had sent to meet me with an imperturbably optimistic driver, Rajan, who seemed to smile and beam more as traffic became heavier and hazards more obvious. I would later regard this as typically Indian: to consider increased burdens as a kind of blessing, as an opportunity to demonstrate that one was even more patient and accepting than one had thought previously, that one could face anything the gods doled out; as an opportunity to show that the god-infused human spirit (like a banyan tree) could triumph against even greater odds, the logos of reincarnation.

But I did not share this optimism as Rajan steered his way around and between water buffalo carts, broken patches of road, squatting and shitting city villagers, begging children who approached the window when we slowed down. I was pleased, if anything pleased me at that moment, to look at the world through a window, and I remember thinking that Orwell had forgotten to mention in his famous example that a window-pane may allow one to see through clearly and to efface the personality of the seer/observer, but it protects, as well.

I was grateful, if a little guilty, that a window and slightly drawn curtain protected me from scalding sun and heat and imploring hands, from having to look at the face of the jasmine-covered corpse who was being carried on some kind of palette along the road toward one or another funereal end. As he doubtless could not afford to live, so he couldn't afford to die, and he would be lucky if his friends found a charitable crematorium for him. Otherwise, he might be floated out to the Bay of Bengal after being dumped where the Ganges turns into the Hooghly.

As much as I had wanted to go to India for three decades, as much as I had wanted to open myself to the spiritually cleansing effect of the legendary subcontinent, I now found myself huddled in the back of the sedan, looking at, and away from, the road, intrigued and appalled by the young bathers who poured buckets of water over themselves as they washed down the water buffalo whose horns glided just above the murky water. For all their openness and nakedness, for all the fusion of man and animal, they were not Whitman's bathers, and I did not feel like celebrating them in poetry.

I slouched in the back as Rajan, inspirited with good cheer, kept saying, as we drove perilously close to the apparently unending procession of women balancing urns and jugs on their heads, "No problem, everything is working just right." I gathered that he meant that the car hadn't broken down, that the police hadn't thrown up a blockade against Sikh terrorists (as they were doing in the Punjab), that Maoist extremists weren't demonstrating (as they were in Hyderabad), that the monsoons hadn't swept us off the road (they were a month away), that we hadn't run over one of the straight-backed women of burden, and that we hadn't run out of gas.

I could see that everything was working just right from his point of view, but I didn't share his perspective. I was a tourist and writer behind, if not under, glass. It was where, somewhat guiltily, I wanted to be and perhaps needed to be. I was an observer and outsider at that moment. Something like self-destruction seemed the only alternative in that moment in a country where life and death are so pressed together that one must be a "passenger" (safely behind glass, or its equivalent) before one can make a "passage."

I had come to India to live, if only for a short while, more openly, to let the infinitude of the cosmos and the soul of the masses wash over me, as if those dual forces had origins in the pure headwaters of the melting Himalayan streams, and now I felt as if I were suffering a fate similar to those streams, as they become contaminated at the polluted confluence of the Ganges and Hooghly. I was no Thoreau, but, then, he hadn't gone to India.

You cannot accept India until you can face death in a way that is alien to an American and Western point of view. Until you have absorbed and believe, in some way, in the great mythologies that affirm life in the midst of death and which in India are embodied in potent god-figures and fertile goddess-images (such as the full-breasted celestial nymphs at the Sun Temple in Konarak), you are unprepared to ride with composure from the airport to the Maidan, the old British parade field in the center of Calcutta.

Until then, you huddle in the back of a sedan and cover your face with a handkerchief to keep out the dust and some of the pollutants and hope you'll survive long enough to have a redeeming vision, to step out from behind the glass, to go outdoors, to give up your preconceptions, to meet life on its own terms, to find out if that's even possible. I was relieved, then, when we emerged from the windings of narrow streets (so narrow as to seem as much footpaths as thoroughfares) into the gate-enclosed courtyard of the New Kenilworth Hotel, where a regimentally dressed doorman took my few bags.

"Just like Sir Walter Scott," Rajan said.

"Yes, of course," I said hesitantly.

If the Raj is dead in India in general and West Bengal in particular, as it clearly is in this Communist-controlled province, where Lenin and St. Theresa, not Clive (c. 1758), are the presiding deities, it has not been properly buried. Remnants are everywhere, not least in the language and the names of things.

Far from the Highlands, far from the nineteenth century, "Kenilworth" has some resonance. And, if anything, "New" means *revived*, not *revised*. The Colonial legacy – especially as it is encapsulated in language – blinds you to what lies before your eyes (unless what you see is the blinkering effect of Colonialism itself), but you are grateful that you feel as if you are in a familiar place, even if that familiarity is only literary and symbolic.

One moves between the great symbolic figures of Hinduism and British Colonialism, feeling safe, confident in one's comprehension of the environment and events, and one wonders at the same time about the obvious disparities between systems of belief and facts of life. Hinduism and Colonialism are like the shabby sedan, with its partly curtained window, that took me from the airport to the New Kenilworth in Calcutta. They clarify and protect. They make observation possible and keep painful truths at a distance. Not unlike writing!

But I was grateful for the misleading anachronism, for the momentary support that the words "New Kenilworth" gave me. If exotic names – such as "Mandalay" and "Kuala Lumpur" – call one to the East and are part of the lure and substance of travel, it is equally true that echoes of the West, even of a disappeared West, are reassuring to the reluctant traveler-writer like myself. I was grateful for the porter and for the obsolete language and for the room whose fans and air-con seemed to be working and for the view down into the courtyard where people, dressed mainly in obligatory white, were sipping required gin and tonics under parti-colored umbrellas.

I was grateful, again, to be behind glass, to look down at the scene as one views photographs (of an unpleasant experience) after a trip: with all the heat and inconvenience left in the developing room, with rain and heat beyond the border of the photograph. I was grateful, but I had not come so far to stay behind glass. I had to go into the streets, where life takes up permanent residence as in all the world's major cities.

Later, at the entrance of the New Kenilworth, an old, bony man stands like a ghostly sentinel next to his rickshaw. He seems to be waiting for me. His eyes light up when we face one another. It is as if we have known one another for years. He *has* known me for years; I am nothing more or less than an "American tourist," a generic entity who means so many rupees to him.

And, I suppose, I know him. He is "suffering man," "the exploited," the "end-product" of Colonialism, a literary icon. I have always known him, but he has never been so concretely embodied. I do not want to make him suffer anymore. I do not want him to haul my body around the Maidan for a few rupees; I do not want to make his rickety legs bow any more. I look away and take a brisk step to the left, but he quickly throws the yoke over his shoulder and rolls the high-wheeled vehicle in stride with me.

"Good ride, ten rupees," he says.

Ten rupees was a little more than a dollar then, but like many tourists, I'm convinced that I'm being taken, hustled. I am on the verge of bargaining, looking sullen and resentful. I almost bark "eight" or "nine" at him, but I catch myself and quicken my pace. I don't want to put his shoulder to the wheel for me.

"Nine," he says, "good ride, Calcutta by night."

"No ride," I say.

"Please, mister," he implores, smiling, beaming, "food for children."

He is doubtless too old to have children, but he is probably a grandfather or a great-grandfather. It doesn't matter in any case. He certainly needs food and is entitled to work for it. If he is going to work like an animal, he can say that the labor is for someone else.

I now knew that I would get up into his rickshaw, put him on the rack of those high wheels, but knowing that I will have to give more than ten rupees. I am spending more than one hundred rupees for a room, twenty rupees for a gin and tonic.

How can I give him ten rupees to haul my body through the streets of Calcutta? But if I am going to give him twenty rupees (twice as much as he has asked for in the arithmetic of need, an equation he will understand), I must ask him to go farther to justify my irrational response.

"Okay," I say, making a wide arc with my arm, "all around for twenty," counting out the number with two gestures of both hands.

He looks at me quizzically and then beams even more, if that is possible. He seems to be positively shining in the late twilight admixture of violet light and dust that characterizes Calcutta before the monsoon season.

He is indifferent to my dilemma: ashamed if I make him haul me around the Maidan, guilty if I deprive him of an evening's earnings. He is trying to eke out another day's existence; I am trying to make sense out of my experience – the typical equation in these matters: academic-intellectual anguish, the writer and the world. As usual, I am riding, sitting in the back of a vehicle, looking at the lantern-lit hawkers' stalls that now fill the street like fireflies.

He picks up speed after a few steps. It is apparently easier for him to move the rickshaw when he moves faster. He has to expend more energy with his lower body to lessen the burden of my weight, another unpleasant equation that makes me want to head back to the hotel and book a flight out of India in the morning.

But there are no return flights to Singapore for several days, and I have obligations to meet in Hyderabad, where I have promised that I will go to meet some students at the

American Studies Research Center. It's one of the caravanserais on the academic trade routes that I had been thinking about for some time.

He takes me past innumerable stalls where families huddle between wares, sleeping in corners behind baskets of produce, cooking as they also try to sell. Life here is naked, exposed. But even at the edge of extinction, they cannot afford to be passive and exhausted, as at home, where people can be marginalized, laid off, put out to pasture, and still go on for years, decades.

I want to touch this life, but I know I must get off the rickshaw, the vehicle that, like Orwell's window, the critic's theory, allows me to gain perspective at a safe distance. I want to test my observations against experience close up.

I hope the old man, now glistening with sweat, will cheat me and take me no farther for twenty rupees than he would have for ten so that I can get back to the hotel, have another gin and quinine water (I remain convinced that quinine will ward off malaria in the tropics). But I dare not say anything; he might think I am complaining and take me even farther, past the Victoria Memorial, around the Race Course.

He ends as he began, beaming, and when I give him twenty-five rupees, he says, "Good ride tomorrow, only fifteen rupees." I see that I am headed for financial ruin if I stay in Calcutta at this hotel. It's a good thing I'll be leaving the next evening before he has a chance to shake, with my help, the last rupees out of my pocket.

I set out in the morning in search of definitive experience, to hear the song of experience, to see the real, the actual, and the human. With map in hand and musty rupees stuffed in my linen pants, I set out in quest of the experience that years of teaching and reading and writing have concealed and displaced.

At the hospice of the destitute and dying, not far from Mother Teresa's Mission of Charity, not far from the Indian Museum and Asiatic Society, I cautiously approach the

80

grillwork of a shadowy entrance. As I stand fearfully at the entranceway, I realize that her worldwide fame as comforter of the desperate and desperately rejected bears little connection to the actual circumstances in which her work, and the work of her order, takes place. This place says both more and less than her "fame" and what she is famous for. It is far more modest, far less impressive as a testament to the possible lessening of pain and suffering, and yet its actuality – a pale and frail body that I now see, lying and moaning along a wall at the place where the hallway seems to become a room, as my eye adjusts to the light – speaks more bitterly and terribly about life and death in India.

Standing by the grillwork, I almost feel relieved, for I have come upon a "scene," if I must use this word, so binding in its facticity, so compelling to the moral sense in its call for redress and a structuring of human history, that I feel as if I have found what I am looking for: a naked encounter with India in the flesh, no window between me and what I see, no vehicle to cart me away.

But what can I do with this one scene, this one response? Am I to devote my life to the study of this one hallway in a shadowy corner of Calcutta? Will I try to show that the historic "black hole" is now a bit of tourist language cut off from whatever "reality" it once named, that the monument commemorating the massacred British troops (1756) cannot compete with the numbers of the living-dying – of which the Mission of Charity is an example and emblem – who make up today the face of Calcutta?

I must go on and look more, even harder, and try to "put together" what I have seen, even if it is impossible to do so. I go to the Kali Temple and stand again in the shadow – not to be seen seeing, watching, to stay out of the pre-monsoon heat that approaches one hundred ten degrees during my "visit," if that is what I can call my trip to India. Here, as everywhere in India, people live in the shadows of the temple and sleep on its ledges, to be able to pray, to stay out of the rain, to be out of harm's way. But here people have an air of expectancy about them, looking furtively and hopefully toward a hallowed, stained slab, which I understand intuitively (and have confirmed later) is a sacrificial table.

I know that these people are waiting to share the remains of the daily sacrifices, and I know that they do this on a daily basis. They constitute something like a class in India, as do beggars. They have institutionalized their misery. I realize in looking at the slab in one attentive moment that I have already forgotten the impact of the hallway at Mother Teresa's Mission, that India will be a succession of such moments, that my perceptions will collide with one another, render each other inadequate. I see that India will present me with an endless succession of fixed images, each of which could lead to an idea, a construction; that one fact in its context will give way to the next; that it will be precisely the knowability of India that will undo my vision, not its mysteriousness or invisibility or hiddenness. I see that the greatest challenge to realism, so to speak, in India is reality itself, a succession of vivid and undeniable moments.

It will not do to agree with Updike, however sympathetic I am toward him, that there is a "real world" and then to set about to try to describe it; and it certainly won't work for me to go along with a contemporary writer who, in a recent one-page summary of postmodernism, says about an artist:

> Then he walked to the real desk, sat down, took out a sheet of paper and began to sketch a picture of himself sitting at the desk sketching himself. (Raymond Federman, *Kiosk,* Vol.3, Winter 88-89, 2)

What lies between "realism" and "irrealism"? Must one choose between presenting the world and re-presenting it? I think, as I have tried to suggest and demonstrate here, that the writer must travel away from his habitual grounds of knowing (including previous literary landscape), get around a bit, get out of the vehicles that have been transporting and protecting him, face specific facts in their contexts; and then repeat this process, however difficult and contradictory, until he can begin to put together one set of facts in context with another set in context, until he has created (recreated?) a world that both does and does *not* exist as we usually talk about these things.

And when he has made (remade) the world in the only way that a writer can – through an act of writing – he must be prepared to leave it as a kind of "scribal embellishment," a specimen in a "collection" for another writer or traveler or reader to come upon to use and put to the test and revise, for he knows that facts shift in relation to context and that contexts shift in relation to one another.

But the writer must remember that humanity continues to cry and cry out in all of this. The moan doesn't go away. His struggle is to hear and understand the moan in all its meaning and implication. It is not enough just to capture the moan, though he must start there. If the writer despairs, it should not be because the world doesn't mean piece by piece, but rather because there is so much meaning, so much to be apprehended, faced, understood, and "put together."

His duty, to use the words of a former student of mine from Sudan, is "to face difficulties in order to be the mind and the tongue for those who were born to suffer, [such as for] my own people in Sudan." Any language, which does not convey, somehow, this suffering, speaks in a false tongue.

Re-vision

India is on the upswing economically. Its IT sector is impressive, and it sends highly qualified students to the US for advanced training. Some return to India and start up "outsourcing centers" in cities such as Bangalore. As a democratic country with a large Moslem population, India, like Turkey, is a country to which the US can look for help and guidance in coming to terms with the revived conflicts between the Islamic and the non-Islamic world, what looks like a neo-Crusade. Thomas Friedman includes India, along with Russia and China, in what he calls the "Axis of Order."

But India remains for me a definitive context of what ordinary people, the man in the street, mean by reality and actuality. No degree of sophistication, if that's what it is, convinces me that reality is, in radically subjective terms, a mere construct. For reasons that defy easy explanation, certain modern and postmodern ideas about the arbitrary nature of existence, personal and social, have shaped academic thinking for several decades. India stood and stands, in my view, as a great counter-example of this privileged form of denial.

An Indian friend, poet and professor of English wrote to me the other day: "But in fact nothing has changed so far: the same poverty, the same rape and murder, the same killing of innocent people, rather more acute problems of unemployment, the increasing gap between the rich and the poor, the same helplessness of individuals, the same price rises, the same sad story of hunger in Kalahandi…." He goes on with a litany of seemingly irremediable problems, even as he acknowledges the advance of the "IT sector."

In my three trips to India (1988, 1990, 1992), I saw little that altered my original impression that India calls one to moral attention; and nothing that I have learned with sustained communication with India friends, writers, and colleagues, leads me to think that I would not be compelled again to look reality in the face and to be tempted to turn away if were I to return.

I keep India in mind as a teacher. I try to be aware of what I call "essentials." I encourage students, where possible, where appropriate, to tell the naked truth in literate terms as an act of self-clarification. In a recent course on Autobiography, I asked students to write their own mini-memoirs and, in so doing, to be as honest as some of the writers whom we had read. Although I had discussed some formal and aesthetic requirements, I did not know what to expect in the way of content.

84

These memoirs revealed a catalogue of dysfunction and courage: anorexia, rape, near poverty, alcoholism, parental abuse, theft, self-mutilation, inter-racial conflict, low self-esteem. These problems and others were proof positive for me that educators in America need to pay attention to the mainstream of life. What we see and hear on "confessional" TV programs, clinical versions of soap operas, turns out to be a reflection of these widespread problems. In a strange way, celebrity can be a by-product of these social failures. One program features a well-known "psychic" who tells her suffering audience how their psychological and spiritual wounds may be healed. Nathaniel West's 1933 *Miss Lonelyhearts* is all too prophetic a novella.

When my department and others in the Humanities search for new faculty, they do not look for young scholars who are interested in social welfare. This is not to say that some of these junior faculty aren't interested in the underside of American life; but if they are, they tend to keep these interests as hidden cards. But if the card does turn up, it's usually in the theoretical form of Marxism which, in its own way, puts the problem outside the self-protective "window" of detached academic "discourse," not real talk. I try to remember the moan when I teach and write. I am not asked to serve on search committees, but, then, few of my colleagues are asked to lecture overseas in places where humanity cries out with unembarrassed need. Still, I am complicit and guilty in some ways for I have not always spoken up about my true feelings in this area, though I have expressed them in writing. Had I written a mini-memoir for my class, this might have been my theme, as it is, in part, in this collection of essays.

CHAPTER SEVEN

FAREWELL
TO HONG KONG:
A CULTURAL VALEDICTORY

My farewell to Hong Kong must be at once an intimate goodbye to a place that I have known and felt in my mind and body and an elegy, of sorts, for a historical-political entity that will cease to exist at midnight on June 30, 1997, and whose future is uncertain.

As everyone who visits Hong Kong knows it from two sides (island and "Kowloon side," one of Hong Kong's many unique locutions), as one sees it crossing Victoria Harbor in two directions on the Star Ferries, so I feel and comprehend its actuality personally and impersonally.

So let me imagine at both levels what I will reimagine at some point in the near future: what prospective retrospective sights, sounds, images, scenes, and words will haunt me during long and cold winter nights in Buffalo, New York, where the glow of lamplight in the hollows of great snowdrifts can provide sometimes a wonderful resting place for historical reverie as well as a chilling sense of loss.

(1) I will reimagine Star Ferry, site and crossings. It's hard to imagine any traveler to Hong Kong, to say nothing of perma-nent resident, who has not plied the waters of Victoria Harbour on Star Ferry; and it's hard to think of any

representation of Hong Kong in which Star Ferry would not figure importantly.

Whether we think of Hong Kong as an entrepot or "contact zone," it's virtually inevitable that we think of it as a go-between culture at various levels. Hong Kong is an in-between place for most people for whom Hong Kong is not natal ground, even if that in-between interval lasts two or three decades. Leaving or staying is a constant question. There is always a sense of exile and wandering in the air. And I imagine that this will continue to be the case "after" Hong Kong becomes part of the People's Republic of China as a Special Autonomous Region, for then memory will be divided, in various ways, with different sets of feelings and beliefs, into "before" and "after". This was the case in the American South after the Civil War and even continues after more than a century and a half.

"Belongers," the affluent as well as the children of the have-nots, think of emigration (60,000 plus or minus 10 percent each year). Lives are suspended on a tightrope between a burgeoning economy and the recurrent challenges of Chinese history – June 4, 1989, the most recent episode. The dragon is always there – sleeping or breathing.

This is one of the reasons (coupled with British reserve and Chinese insularity within the family) why social relations are precarious for the visitor, even the sojourner of some duration: people are cautious about making connections and affiliations in this society; people are wary of adding unknown elements to the chemistry of their social existence.

Liaisons are another matter. Sudden collisions and entanglements are the predictable reverse side of the international coin here. Strangers reach out in the nightclub districts of Lan Kwai Fong and Wanchai; and a panoply of escort services serve to assuage their cultural isolation, to ease their "sexual loneliness" (in the words of one candid traveler between worlds). Sometimes, a person from Dry Gulch (separated) in America may meet someone (divorced) from Penang in Hong Kong, and they may decide, against cultural odds, to try for a new life on the Gulf of Mexico. Gulfs look better than abysses at a certain point in life, especially on a moonlit night on the Peak, Hong Kong's famed elevation.

And quite often, a lonely, aging bachelor (usually a corporate manager on an expat's allowance) will find a younger Chinese woman to be his life's companion as it moves toward the end game. One of these "blokes" said to me in a bar one night that he had found his "Ming-thing" after many years of boozing and whoring. Concubines may be part of the past, but "strangers in the night" is another thing.

Each crossing of the ferry reminds us – if not all the time, then one by one and sometimes cumulatively – that Hong Kong's history will be divided categorically in two after June 30, 1997; that the lives of expatriates in Hong Kong are divided between here and a home elsewhere (even if that home is held in abeyance for decades), a possible and plausible place of return: Lake District, Sydney, Vancouver, San Francisco, Isle of Skye, and even Buffalo, New York, my lakeport of safe call.

The crossings are pleasant in their brevity, and so we approach them casually, let down our mental guard; and, letting down our guard, we allow ourselves to think of our own life's journey, the crossings we have made (for better and worse), the ones we failed to make (the missed turn, the unlived life), and the voyages that lie ahead. The mini-sea voyages on the Star Ferries allow us to contemplate the Right and Left Banks of our lives, if not brains, and to take the measure of lost opportunity, as well as the possibility for renewal.

Each crossing is a small surrender – to memory, the flow of thought – and a return to safe ground: culture, shopping, commerce, companionship; but it is the surrender, I think, that will be missing in the years to come for those ex–Hong Kong people who don't live on active seaports; and, even then, few ports can rival Hong Kong's perpetual motion and light show.

I shall miss a feeling of what I call "magisterial adulthood," fleeting, to be sure, on certain mid-autumn evenings when everything seemed right: temperature, light wind, transfiguration of neon into Monet-like pastel watery reflections, when I felt that I had become all that I wished to be; and I shall also recall the attendant sadness, the recognition that some sense of shortfall would come with landfall, for after all, "at the end of the day" (favored Hong Kong idiom), such poetic reverie usually cannot be sustained in the midst of society.

(2) I shall reimagine sitting at my computer screen, loyal, constant companion, looking through the sliding glass doors of my high-rise apartment beyond Mount Davis across the harbor to Kowloon, the New Territories, and, on a clear day, China. The harbor itself is a study of composure and motion, hundreds of still ships lying-to at anchor, hundreds of others in constant and seemingly random motion, the yin and yang of commercial life in Hong Kong. The harbor, in this doubleness, is an emblem of Hong Kong's relentless enterprise and its ability, despite its expenditure of mercantile energy, to pursue a steady course, to maintain a sense of (dare I say Confucian?) calm in the midst of a fierce market-driven economy.

This doubleness is visible in the ladder-streets leading down to Kennedy Town and Central, in the thousands of "holes in the walls," where small operators have found a niche for themselves: carefully carved out and protected commercial spaces that, collectively, cry out against theories of entropy and loss of energy.

When a politically correct colleague in Buffalo asked me before I came out to Hong Kong why I wanted to go to such a center of "predatory capitalism," I should have said, but didn't know enough to say, "Because it lets people accept responsibility for their own lives, and it lets the individual work for the family. Can you think of a higher ethic for a Chinese person? Would you prefer sado-masochistic socialism?" I hoped, before I left, that this spirit would continue in significant ways after 1997, and this seems to be the case.

My window-view is also a point of view. The weather is visible, sweeping mist and rain, usually from West to East, in constantly shifting patterns that symbolically reverse the direction of contemporary history. The patterns remind us of human and historical mutability; and, as I look to the hills beyond, to the trail of lights following the line of the KCR (Kowloon Canton Railroad) beyond Beacon Hill, I wonder, with everyone else in Hong Kong, about the future of this (what shall we call it?) Crown Colony ... Territory ... Special Administrative Region ... stillborn Republic ... entrepot ... collection of Hong Kong people ....

No one can predict the future of Hong Kong – any more or less than Kremlinologists were able to see beyond the fall of the Iron Curtain in 1991 – but this much is clear: after June 30, 1997, Hong Kong will be cut off from its British colonial past and rejoined, in some fashion, with a motherland (dominated by male "paramount" leaders) whose future is precarious and unpredictable.

Everyone outside Hong Kong asks, what will happen to Hong Kong after 1997? But the questions really should be: what will happen to and in China after 1997, after the death of Deng? What will happen if the bamboo gulag *(laogai)*, with its alleged 20,000,000 "forced laborers," is ever torn down? Future-gazers and prognosticators need to look into the right crystal ball, for starters.

In this sense, Hong Kong is an emblem, again, of our lives, as we look back to past lives we cannot retrieve and futures we cannot predict. But those of us who live as more or less free individuals in nations that embrace versions of liberty will be able to make choices about the kind of future we would like to make for ourselves; Hong Kong people – those who stay (most) – will be playing at the gaming table of history. But, of course, Hong Kong people like to gamble. One nation's Elysian Fields is another's Happy Valley racecourse.

(3) As I reimagine *my* "lost city," not Scott Fitzgerald's, I shall recall moments and enclaves of civility within the hurly-burly and brusque rhythms of Hong Kong's daily life. There are moments of stillness and decorum here that may not be visible to the casual visitor or tourist.

I shall reimagine the courtyards of the Main Building at the University of Hong Kong, especially the one outside my office, in mid-February, when yellow jasmine and rose rhododendron bloom, where the odd orange carp flashes in the occasional sun this time of year, as a site of civility and calm within an often machine-like system where the pressure of the year-end examinations has the force of fate whose meaning and purpose our good students do not question, at least openly.

I shall recall this courtyard as an oasis of tranquility through which students, mainly women, sometimes my students, move, but never rush, even when they are in a hurry. In all situations and at all times, University of Hong Kong students (perhaps all Chinese students in traditional settings) may quicken their pace and take many accelerated short steps, but they do not break into a run. Some restraining force is at work, some code of decorum that prevents an intrusive and aggressive gesture.

I have wondered sometimes if these short steps are a legacy of bound feet, of following behind men who are moving at a faster pace with whom they must not appear to catch up, but then I realize that it is the same for the young men in the Arts Faculty, a small percentage, but a percentage nonetheless, unless it's possible that the young men, so outnumbered, are imitating the young women.

On the face of it, Hong Kong would seem to be more traditional than the Mainland in a number of ways; and it certainly seems true that University of Hong Kong students are more mannered than their cousins to the north. Hong Kong certainly takes the cake for bridal gowns, formal weddings, and ceremonial photographs. It is not unusual to see a Rolls-Royce, festooned with balloons and lilies, waiting to take a young couple to the first destination of their life's journey; and one believes – looking at the pride of the brides – that it will be for life.

I see these manners at work when papers are handed out for distribution in the classroom. If a sheaf of papers is handed to a student, s/he will take one sheet discreetly from the bottom and pass on the packet; but, if the teacher hands out the papers a sheet at a time, the student will reflexively pass it on until there is no one left to take a sheet except the first student.

Such small matters count in the observation of all cultures, but it may be fair to say that the observation of small moments matters more in an Asian context, where, we might say, the micro-level of organization and action is taken as seriously (perhaps more seriously) than the macro-level (the American specialty). I say this even as I am fond of saying that "China may have the Great Wall, but Hong Kong has the Great Mall," even as Hong Kong's new buildings (Bank of China, Central Plaza) pierce the sky as pointedly as the great towers of New York and Toronto; but even here, we might say that Hong Kong's apparent architectural giantism is a function of the island's compactness, of the late triumph of market forces and property values over a historical propensity to operate efficiently in small spaces. Or we can say that both levels of organization and action are at work in Hong Kong.

As my students take small steps and stow all their writing and examination implements in small school-boxes (often imitations or remnants of lower-school objects, including Disney decorations), so Hong Kong people will universally press the "close" button when they enter an elevator or begin to ascend the steps of a bus.

The impulse to save time and money – like the use of what I call the weapons of trade: pager, calculator, cell-phone, PC/notebook – is, at one level, a form of reducing the scale of operations. The three-martini lunch (American-style) is replaced by the three-minute cell-phone conversation; the instantaneous "bye-bye" at the end of a transaction is the Hong Kong equivalent of the lingering conversation at the door at the end of an American party.

Compared to Hong Kong, America is now a slow and pastoral (as it is, of course, also a violent) country. In ways both positive and negative, to go from Hong Kong to America, especially the part I call home (western New York) is to go from an emergent century to a fading one. The end of the American empire is catching up with Britain's descent. The dollar and pound are uneasy bedfellows against the yen and the increasing value of the yuan.

As America lost many of its manners in a breakneck effort to make it in the twentieth century, it remains to be seen whether Hong Kong, the Tigers, the Pacific Rim, and a new China can surface as the dominant economic powers in the world with some decorous traditions intact. If not, this moment in Hong Kong will become even more magical in the years to come: a historical interval when traces of old Chinese civility – such as the formal exchange of name and business cards, a moment of calm and ethical respect for the existence of the other in the midst of the most frenzied activity – were still felt in the vortex of what F. Scott Fitzgerald calls a "golden boom."

In fact, what Fitzgerald says further about the America of 1919 in his "Early Success" might be said with some substitutions about Hong Kong today: "America was going on the greatest, gaudiest spree in history and there was going to be plenty to tell about. The whole golden boom was in the air – its splendid generosities, its outrageous corruptions, and the tortuous death struggle of the old America..."

Today, the world admires Japan and Hong Kong. Hong Kong's menus and venues make everyone with a holiday bankroll feel like a page or some kind of royal in the court of one of the Bourbons or Hollywood's version of the late Roman Empire. Any tourist can revisit Babylon on a package tour. If such cultures are not resented for their luxury in the short term, they often work against themselves eventually. The children of immigrants become merchants and entrepreneurs; their children become professionals; and their children, in turn, often seek fashionable and easy lives (with or without gainful employment, with or without parental support).

But I don't see these patterns yet among my students in the Arts Faculty at the University of Hong Kong. Mainly daughters of the working and emergent middle class, they are hard-working, disciplined, and cordial, if sometimes unimaginative (or required to be so by a British system that puts so much emphasis on examinations and rankings). They have followed a tortuous path of exams leading to the A-levels, and they don't want to deviate from the main road. These students do not take education for granted, unlike many of their American counterparts. They are, if anything, too polite. They never enter an office without a polite knock; all paper is handed to you with two hands – nothing is ever thrust at you; and these graceful students present their teachers with cards of appreciation at the end of the term. Tradition may or may not shape the meaning of respect here. What's important for the moment is that Hong Kong students have not yet been sidetracked by a culture of luxury, but it's out there as a temptation.

It may be the case that Hong Kong's uncertain and probably difficult future – at least over the next decade – will keep the society sufficiently focused on essentials and necessities so that the spree won't get out of hand. At this point in its history, Hong Kong U. students still look their lecturer in the eye and take notes along a straight line without lowering their heads.

(4) I will reimagine Chater Road and Chater Garden on Sundays, the epicenter of festivals and charity events of a colonial cast and seat of government (the Legislative Council, LEGCO – arguably the most important building in the world at the moment: where capitalism debates and contemplates its encounter with one of the last bastions of "socialism"). It is also the gathering place and collection point for tens of thousands of mainly Filipina housekeepers (usually called "amahs" in this part of the world).

These women come together on this day of rest on these streets (and under the Hong Kong Shanghai Bank) to share music, food, and photographs and to chat from morning until night because they have few other places to go in a city that, essentially, welcomes them only as workers, not people with a complicated sets of needs.

There are some men among these women – hawkers and traders from Pakistan, India, and the Middle East, and some Filipino workers (mainly musicians) – but the essential atmosphere here is one of good-natured women making the best of a bad situation: Unable to make a living at home commensurate, in many cases, with advanced education, these women have come to Hong Kong because of the relatively high level of wages.

The people of Hong Kong do not, generally speaking, respect these women, even though they have entrusted the care of their infants and children to them so that they (working mothers and fathers) can devote themselves full time and fully to the marketplace in a city where the fluctuations of the Hang Seng index are as important as the vital signs of one's body.

The Filipinas have become a defacto subject people in a city that respects only (in the main) success, profit, family values (including prosperity); and Hong Kong people who are apprehensive about domination from the North have little, if any, self-consciousness, to say nothing of guilt, about dominating these women from the Philippines who provide most of the good music in this territory. They generate energy in the midst of relative commercial calm on Sundays – the opposite of the Hong Kong Chinese state of the psyche during the working week, where poise is maintained in the center of the vortex, to wit, the quiet on the floor of the Hang Seng stock exchange.

Every mature culture needs both sides (commerce challenging art, complex human needs calling materialism into question), but I do not sense, despite some human generosity in Hong Kong's recent budgets, that the magnates of the Midlevels appreciate the actual as well as symbolic contribution of the Filipina community.

It must be said in fairness that British law and a solid Chinese sense of human decency see to it that these housekeepers are protected by social welfare guidelines and Department of Labor regulations.

There are examples of exploitation – sweatshops, harsh treatment – but the indignities are mainly moral and psychological: the reduction of a people to racial and national stereotypes that have been so common in world history; and, as one might predict, the Filipina women are thought to be "unclean," "primitive," "prostitutes" by the same people, again, who entrust them with the cleanliness of their own homes.

Because they have nowhere else to go, they inevitably litter the streets after a day of congregation. They thus become "unclean"; and Western businessmen who seek them out in the bars of Wanchai (another site of gathering) to assuage their sexual loneliness think of them as "fallen."

The people of Hong Kong have demonstrated considerable genius over the past century and a half of British rule, but it has been applied to a narrow economic sphere. The treatment of the amahs, the failure to find a more humane approach to a social problem, is a case in point; and this failure to appreciate a people who add a measure of soul to the golden bowl of commerce may suggest why, in part, Hong Kong's future is endangered.

No one, except, perhaps, the diplomats who cut deals, can say with certainty how Hong Kong may best protect itself in the future; but it would seem clear that the liberal voices of Martin Lee, Emily Lau, and Christine Loh, to say nothing of Chris Patten, and those who will follow them will not carry the day against the mega-scale of China's power without a chorus of powerful voices in the economic sector joining them. I have not heard the billionaires speak out in defense of Hong Kong's rights. And I assume that their inheritors will keep discreet silence on key divisive issues in the future. Power speaks the same language all over the world, though dialects may differ. The tycoons and taipans are mainly silent; they are hedging their bets and watching their assets. They are not concerned about the amahs of Central, and they may not be concerned about human rights and liberties.

So I will reimagine Central on Sundays in the years to come as a crucible of Hong Kong's moral imagination – an emblem of short-sightedness in a legendary place that could have become a state only through a more profound belief in human diversity and through a willingness to pay a price to defend and protect that diversity. In an irony that might be lost on Hong Kong people, I will think of the fate of the amahs as parallel with the fate of Hong Kong itself.

(5) I will think of the Cenotaph ("The Glorious Dead: 1914–1918, 1939–1945") in the shadow of the Bank of China with its spires of aspiring dominance: a fading world and an emerging one; site of homage to those who fell to defend the Territory under the British flag. I shall think of some colonial types, short-sighted sons and daughters of Britain who did not possess the wisdom – until too late in the day – to secure, somehow, in perpetuity the autonomy of this remarkable community. I shall think in particular of one Brit, age fifty, married to a Hong Kong Chinese woman, with a high-paying civil service job, who drinks too much and has spent too much time at the Ladies Recreation Club. This person, who has lived and worked in Hong Kong for twenty-five years, who no longer feels at home in England and may not be welcome after 1997, who has helped sustain the rule of law here, whatever else may be said of him, did not see early enough what needed to be done, if anything could have been done, to protect Hong Kong.

Another Brit, Oxford educated, who teaches English Renaissance literature in the Chinese University, refuses to believe that the students who enter the university after 1997 may not be interested in *la tradition anglaise*. He came out to this Crown Colony thirty years ago, he insists, not to preach the values of Empire but to defend literature against philistinism wherever it appears. His Hong Kong, Taiwan, and overseas Chinese colleagues have been trying to get him to shift his interests somewhat in order to preserve a viable place for him after 1997; they are not wholly insensitive to the fate of expats who have given their lives to this place. He is intransigent.

"Let the place go to hell," he says privately. "If teaching Shakespeare means bringing in the tanks, so be it."

He has fewer and fewer people to speak to these days. There are several possible futures for Hong Kong, but this overseas teacher fits into none of them. He is, for better and worse, a museum piece. Nonetheless, he stands, in some way, for everything the PRC threatens: the right to lead one's own life in however peculiar a fashion.

But perhaps real autonomy (beyond the theoretical fifty years as a Special Autonomous Region, written into the Joint Sino-British Agreement of 1984) will come in time anyway. I would like to think that one possibility for Hong Kong after 1997, though it would not come immediately, would be the emergence of a joint HK-Guangdong Province as a political as well as economic reality that would make Hong Kong part of a truly autonomous region while satisfying nationalist desires on both sides of the border.

This would only be possible if China were to become, in time, a confederation of regions. This is not an unimaginable configuration in light of the partial experience of post–Soviet Union. Then Hong Kong would find a new history between the Giant Panda to the north and the on-off expatriate Babylon of the South China Sea. At the same time, the PRC is not the former Soviet Union. Beijing's leaders are more likely to seek pragmatic ways to make their ultimate control of Hong Kong clear without interfering in its dynamic economy and without making Hong people feel that their basic rights are being denied.

Just as Beijing allows a candlelight vigil for Tienanmen on June 4, so it is likely to be unobtrusive in other ways, ways that will lead to something like a seamless transition. The new futuristic airport is more likely to become a symbol of the post-British Hong Kong than the motionless PRC guards one is likely to see standing at attention at the former HMS Tamar. As Beijing now tolerates Falun Gong protesters at the entrance to the Star Ferry line and doesn't remove posters depicting punishment suffered by fellow members, so Beijing is likely to let Hong Kong conduct business as usual – and business is at the heart of life in Hong Kong and sometimes rivals the heart.

If Hong Kong becomes "only" one major piece in the puzzle of China, then I will reimagine with nostalgia another colonial composite of an honorable daughter or son of Britain laying a wreath at the base of the Cenotaph to commemorate lives lived and given honorably for an entity that no longer exists. But this monument may itself be moved in time, or disappear.

At the end of "My Lost City," Fitzgerald goes to the observation tower of the Empire State Building and discovers "that the city was not the endless succession of canyons that he had supposed but that *it had limits*." Hong Kong's limits are ones of time, rather than space, though geography comes into it. Everyone knows that the clock is ticking, and everyone is counting. At the same time, it may be true that most people (including the leaders in Beijing) live and act as if Hong Kong's increasing prosperity were limitless. With this belief, really a faith, the people of Hong Kong may not have made it clear that they do not wish prosperity at any price; but perhaps they do.

I am not saying that the old revolutionary standard of New Hampshire should be raised – "Live Free or Die" – but it seems clear that Beijing believes, as it recruits more and more "advisors," that the people of Hong Kong will not take a stand. Should Beijing act as if only the British and a handful of expatriates care about human rights and liberties – about that taboo word "democracy"? But Beijing may be surprised after 1997 to discover that the people of Hong Kong really do have a culture of their own, a culture that has grown accustomed to the face of freedom in all sorts of unspoken ways. Indeed, the people of Hong Kong may be surprised to learn this about themselves.

I will not be here to light candles with my students. But in my mind's eye I shall always hoist the standard of a country that never existed – The Republic of Hong Kong – which, for better and worse, showed the world that grace under pressure was possible for over more than a century and a half (1841–1997) of difficult history from the time of Captain Charles Elliot to the lowering of the Union Jack.

Re-vision

When I arrived in Hong Kong in late August of 1991 to take up a post as a lecturer in American literature and was told that the department would teach John Stuart Mill's *On Liberty* (1859) in the first course, I was somewhat puzzled. It seemed an excessively difficult task to me for students whose first language was not English. But I was assured by the late Piers Gray, T.S. Eliot scholar and playwright, that they could handle it and that, in any case, it would be an important text for them "in the years to come."

I assumed then, without giving it much thought, that he meant it would be an important part of their cultural development, their assimilation to British culture. After all, Piers was a Cambridge man, and it became clear after a while, that he was unembarrassed by some Tory tendencies. Looking back, I can see that Piers, who was deeply committed to freedom of speech as a dramatist and anti-Stalinist, had something else in mind as well: the ability of our students to defend their basic rights of self-expression, among other rights, through their ability to express themselves both in English and Chinese.

The opening sentences of Mill's prophetic book chart a political course for what became one of the major challenges of the twentieth century: to define "the nature and limits of the power which can be legitimately exercised by society over the individual" and to defend the rights of "internal culture," the private and inviolate space of the individual. My students in American Literature, especially a devoted group of students, whom I came fondly to call the "core," embraced these values over the period of my three years in Hong Kong (I graduated, so to speak, with them).

When they saw me off at the old Kai Tek Airport as I bid farewell to them, but *sans adieu* (I promised that I would return at some point), we held onto each other in a tender circle, a surprising show of emotion within Chinese culture. I knew that we were holding onto a small world we had created within the system of Hong Kong University inside the society of Hong Kong on the edge of the soon-to-expand circle of China.

I had encouraged them to speak in their individual voices through our study of American literature with its special emphasis on first-person expression in versions of the autobiographical mode. In holding onto each other, we were embracing as well our mutual recognition of each other as individuals. Mill's work had become a living presence for us. In that instant, we seemed to be British, American, and Chinese all at once within the special atmosphere of Hong Kong, where it wasn't unusual for people to express themselves in festive ways at odd moments.

I am pleased to hear recently from one of the "core" that it is "not less free nowadays."

Another former student, now a teacher of English, more embattled, says that he and his friends want to honor the great tradition of Anglo-American liberalism; and he says, somewhat heroically, "We know what we are fighting for." Another student, always the most independent in the group, is studying international law at a Canadian university after a decade of working in the Commonwealth to earn enough money for her professional education.

A true Hong Konger, she would not take money from her father, whose hierarchical values she had rejected. She wanted, as she once wrote to me, to take the "road not taken of the Robert Frost poem that we studied together." She wishes to return to Hong Kong with her degree and eventually to become a member of LEGCO. Raised on the "outlying island" of Lantau, where she once told me she could see Hong Kong's

Central District glittering in the distance, she still sees it as a place "glittering with possibilities for freedom," as she said to me in a recent e-mail.

Looking back, I now see Hong Kong as an emblem of the struggle of individuals, a group of people, or a social-political entity, to defend their right to existence and self-determination against the imposition of external standards. I explore some of these rights in the essay on South Africa in this collection; and I have explored what I might call "threats to existence" in other recent essays.

I could not predict Hong Kong's future in the past, and I don't think anyone can predict it now, but it seems clear to me through the voices of the "core" that the spirit of liberty will continue to be heard, whatever the implications of that chorus may be. And it is looks as if Hong Kong will serve as a center of literary activity in English over the coming decades. In the language of the *International Herald Tribune* (March 25-26, 2006): "There is nowhere else in the rest of Asia with a market for literature like this. English is the lingua franca of Asia."

So: even as Hong Kong responds to the growing influence of mainland culture, the very need of the PRC to have English as a language for commerce and international relations makes the British (and I might add Anglo-American) legacy all the more important. It may be no more possible to imagine Hong Kong as separate from China than one might try to imagine the Island of Manhattan as a city state separate from the United States of America; but it may be possible to imagine that Hong Kong will, in the fullness of time, have as much influence on greater China as New York does on the information, artistic, and financial center of America.

Having lived for many years in Buffalo, near Niagara Falls, as far away from New York City as Taiwan is from Hong Kong, but always feeling the influence of the city, I take some comfort in the role my former students may play in the future development of China. But I need to be realistic. To a large extent, Hong Kong is now a great city among great cities, including Beijing and Shanghai, whose power and influence can be measured by the current market value of the Bank of China.

The Bank of China is now second only to Citigroup in terms of assets; and Hong Kong's billionaires now look to IPOs listed on the Hong Kong (Stock) Exchange as the Chinese government formerly looked to Hong Kong's shares. Hong Kong has lost, to some extent, its preeminence on the Pacific Rim, but it remains powerful, if a little crestfallen. An overseas Chinese anthropologist, raised in New York, who lives in Hong Kong, recently wrote to me and compared the people of Hong Kong to the people of "Yelang," a proud minority who were overshadowed finally by the Han Chinese.

But he may overstate the case slightly. Another friend, a financial journalist, writes that the main changes have been mainly "symbolic": PRC flags instead of the British Lion; PRC National Day instead of the Queen's Birthday; no bank notes or stamps with the Queen's image; the "deletion" of "Royal" and "Crown" from the names of organizations. Still, he senses the "deeper longings for universal suffrage and political reform and mechanisms to bring them about here."

If Hong Kong has lost some of its centrality, my former students will remember our time together as a high point of a certain kind like America in 1929 – a boom period of high expectations. The next time we meet in the Central District, we will feel closer than ever because we will share a sense of displacement, however private, however symbolic.

That is one of the major themes of this collection. Some losses, looked at from a certain point of view, can become gains.

CHAPTER EIGHT

STARBOARD OUT, PORT HOME:
TOWARD A GLOBAL EDUCATION

I returned to America from Hong Kong via Germany in order to give a lecture in Frankfurt. For an American of my generation, born and raised in New York City during the late 1930s and the war years, Germany evoked memory and feeling at the deepest levels of the mind and psyche; and nothing I could say anywhere could matter more to me than what I might say in Germany a half-century after the disasters of war.

This U.S. Embassy program in Frankfurt marked for me the near conclusion of a kind of pedagogic circumnavigation that began in 1956–57 when I took a leave of absence from Amherst College for a *wanderjahr* in Europe, my first departure from American soil. It was also a sort of homecoming in several senses.

That inaugural trip represented my first exposure to, and experience of, European culture; and, though the war in Europe made the idea of European culture problematic for my generation, it left intact, somehow, a certain substratum of belief in the Classical-Medieval-Renaissance legacy that could be observed firsthand only on the continent. I didn't think of myself as a traveler or teacher in those days (or as someone who might write about the relationship between traveling and learning), so I didn't think of the trip as part of a pattern. It was simply my "year abroad," as we still called such experiences in those Euro-centric days. It wasn't until a quarter of a century later, when I went to Ankara, Turkey, to teach in 1983–84 as a Fulbright lecturer of American literature in Ankara University, that I thought of myself, after a while, as moving East: from North America to Europe to Asia Minor and then the Far East.

It occurred to me then, perhaps that I was reversing on a private and microscopic scale the direction of Columbus's voyage and what had seemed to be the inevitable westering impulse of post-Renaissance history – the discovery (contact) and settlement of the Americas. I was, within this larger pattern, reversing the direction of my grandfather Jacob's flight from Czarist Russia in 1906 when he sailed steerage class for what he and so many millions of immigrants thought of as the promised land.

My grandfather never left America again, rarely mentioned Europe (though he might have, if I had spoken Yiddish or if he had spoken American English better), and he would have been puzzled, if he had been alive, why I, a New York Jew, was returning to the old world, especially a Moslem version of it. My grandfather lived in a kosher and Jewish orthodox world, American-style (Catskill Mountains Hotel Resorts in the summer, Miami Beach in the winter). He tried as much as possible to keep his ritual life separate from the secular influences of New York City and the whole of America.

In retrospect, I am puzzled that he was so apparently unaffected by America over the course of his lifetime and that I remained so seemingly distant from the cultural and religious influences that had shaped him during my youth and early manhood. There is no doubt that my grandfather Jacob would have thought my reentry into the Ottoman world a strange and risky enterprise for a grandson who enjoyed the safe and privileged life of an American middle-class upbringing.

Who knows what he would have made of my going to Kuala Lumpur in 1988 as a lecturer of American literature and American studies in my home university's (SUNY/Buffalo) Malaysian Program. He would certainly have had some ironic Yiddish expression for it, which, roughly translated, would have said, "What?! Are you crazy? Moslems, again." But Malaysia was more than Moslem to me. It was Southeast Asia, part of the Indonesian archipelago, a remnant the old British Empire, and an introduction to Chinese and Indian cultures, given the ratios of ethnic population in Malaysia.

And I hardly can imagine what he might have said when I visited India in 1988 (the first of three visits) and came to teach in Hong Kong in 1991, from where I traveled out to lecture in Korea, Thailand, China, India, the Philippines, Taiwan, and Japan: "Hindus. Buddhists, now. What are you, crazy?"

My grandfather was a pious and simple man; he was also uneducated, provincial, and outside the American mainstream. He would not have understood what I might call the reversal of history and the reglobalization of the world for some Americans of my generation and the generations that followed. My generation was beginning to understand that the world really *is* round. The first globalization was navigational and expansive, an extension of Europe by any means; the second would be electronic and cultural. Ideas, as well as coins, would circulate. Possibilities of synthesis as well as conquest of markets and peoples would emerge.

My grandfather left a Europe (Lithuania) in which he had failed to find a safe niche and a Europe that had failed over the centuries to accept fully the Jewish people. At the same time, he never really found a realization of his dreams in America, if he had them: the streets were not paved with gold; it was not the promised land. In fact, he lived in a tenement on the Lower East Side on the edge of Chinatown and raised five sons and a daughter in poverty: but he was not oppressed, and he lived in modest comfort after his first-born son became affluent enough to take care of him; and he took pride in grandchildren who became lawyers, teachers, writers, and doctors.

His life was a typical tale for most immigrants of his generation, a veritable archetype of American culture: the Irving Berlin story writ small. Neither Horatio Alger nor Willy Loman, he found a place, however modest, in America, the first safe place his people had found since ... who knows when? My grandfather did not look back. Europe and the nineteenth century, the life of the "pale of settlement," were shrouded in darkness; over an ocean he had crossed to enter the twentieth century in America. He would not have understood a grandson who wanted to see the world and who came to believe that several important reversals of world consciousness had taken place (or needed to take place).

Europe still represented civilization and high culture, however problematized these values had become in the aftermath of World War II, for my generation. The world beyond Europe was another matter. The rest of the world, especially Africa and Asia, had served, as many writers and critics have made clear in the past two decades, as playgrounds for the Western imagination (or fantasy-life). Throughout the nineteenth century, Western writers imposed what they took to be their sophisticated ideas and artistic designs upon the alleged primitive, exotic, and irrational landscapes (geographic, moral, social) of these far-away places.

It never quite occurred to Melville, Flaubert, Twain, Conrad, and Kipling that North America, Great Britain, and Europe were as far away from the rest of the world as the rest of the world was from New York, London, and Paris. As Greenwich set the Mean Time, so it determined terra incognito: culture was a one-way trade route; the raw materials of literary production were outsourced "somewheres East of Suez" and manufactured (turned into sophisticated goods) in the mental mills of Boston and Berlin.

Later, of course, these materials became part of Hollywood's repertoire. Empires and epochs, cultures and civilizations – these became grist for the fantasy-mill. The major movie studios of the 1920s and 1930s determined the significance and look of the past for Americans who might never get further than Altoona, Pa., but who would be confident, nonetheless, that they understood the old worlds.

It was doubtless felt that these civilizations were better preserved on the silver screen than they had been or would be in their original contexts. Look at the Acropolis, after all; it was only a ruin. It needed Hollywood's reconstruction to give its fragments meaning. (I have to admit here that when I first saw the ruins of Ephesus in 1984 and the Acropolis in 1990 they seemed to be more ruined than I had imagined; Hollywood had prepared me for something else – not "walls in holes"). For my generation, China was *Charlie Chan;* India, *Gunga Din;* the Holy Land, well, we could take our pick of stars as prophets. And it was even felt that the artifacts of the Greco-Roman world (Aegean and Mediterranean cultures) were somehow safer in the museum preserves of London, Paris, Boston, and Berlin. The Elgin Marbles, the Hearst collection of attic vases in New York's Metropolitan Museum of Art, and German holdings of the ancient coastal sites of Turkey illustrate this point.

My father, who visited one city in Europe to see some grandchildren, said to me, "Why go to Malaysia? It's the armpit of America."

"But Pop," I said, "it's not in America."

"Well, it's an armpit anyway."

So much for innocent cultural arrogance. My generation was beginning to understand, however late in the day, that an appropriate model for world learning is not what we take out and bring back (or import in one form and export in another), but what we may be able to share.

If the old model still works at the level of trade, it's even truer there that transfer of technologies, joint ventures, and other cooperative schemes have replaced simplistic notions of capitalist enterprise; and when it comes to the financing of international projects (industrial, military, and humanitarian), it's increasingly difficult to disentangle New York from Hong Kong, Beijing, and the IMF. But the sharing-model only can take place in an important way when we become consciously aware of what cultural baggage we're carrying with us on the journey out. Only then can we figure out what to discard, what to buy, what to do without on the way back.

I want to list three intellectual and temperamental assets (and their attendant liabilities) that I believe an enlightened, but still culture-bound, American teacher takes out to the world.

(A) An American teacher usually has a commitment, in some fashion, to what I might call the creative individual. An American teacher believes that the individual-learner (to use something of an exhausted phrase) is a reservoir of potential. If the student seems to be motionless in still water, it is a result, such an American teacher may think, of the student's talents having been dammed up by a series of inhibitions. This attitude has roots in American political history, Emersonian Transcendentalism, the educational theories of John Dewey, and modern depth psychology (which took such deep roots in America after Freud's famous visit to the New World in the first decade of this century) – to say nothing of atmospheric notions of frontier individualism, cowboy-independence (Hollywood-style), and post-war Existentialist ideas (America's most important import from France after the penchant for French cuisine and wine in the wake of the 1939 World's Fair, when Henri Soule showed America what French tables and labels looked like).

The negative side of this attribute is the quotient of fantasy that often goes along with it. Both the student and the teacher are likely to misread the student's talents. The teacher may insist on seeing quality where it is lacking; and the students may think that anything that enters their heads (including daydreams) deserves respect and high grades.

(B) American students are suspicious of authority. They do not assume that teacher knows best, or, in extreme cases, that teacher knows anything at all (and there is some discouraging evidence to suggest that this is so in some cases). American students are encouraged from birth to think for themselves and to question the wisdom of the elders. Parents tell children early on to accept responsibility for their lives and to solve their own problems. My own mother often used to tell my brother and me that she was raising us, so to speak, "to fly the coop." She would say this with an admixture of pride, sadness, conviction, and cultural necessity. I did not doubt, from an early age, that my mission in life was, in some important sense, to leave home; and I did. Occasionally, my aged mother now questions the wisdom of her own commitment, but, finally, she believes she did the right thing.

On the positive side, American children do learn to be independent, and, later in life, some wonderful achievements in business, art, and science can result from this early training in self-realization. But there's also a risk – the risk of a break with tradition and all that goes along with it: cultural continuity, a steering mechanism for behavior, and a sense, ultimately, of belonging to a civilization (for which there can be no personal substitute). Civilization is only possible when knowledge and custom can be transmitted from generation to generation in some usable way.

Needless to say, America's early break from Europe and its revolutionary aftermath inaugurated a "tradition of the new" and established patterns of rebellion, though it needs to be remembered that these early departures took place within a framework of orthodoxy and convention. Powerful restraining forces were at work in Puritan New England and pre-Revolutionary British America. The situation is quite different today. American children often invent their own rules of behavior; and it even may be suggested that their acts of rebellion need to be interpreted as a cry for restraint.

To some extent, America's problem is complicated because the mass media (TV and movies) often project sentimental versions of social cohesion (however framed by violence) that serve to camouflage real failures of coherence in American life.

(C) American children, especially children of the middle class, demand authenticity within family relationships. Established roles do not suffice. The nomenclature and role of "father" and "mother" are not sufficient to guarantee respect. Respect must be earned, particularly as the American youngster approaches the teenage years and is in the throes of Erikson's "identity crisis." During this stage and phase of development, American teenagers will scrutinize their parents closely in order to determine if they are capable of meaningful and mutual exchanges. If the adolescent decides or feels that his parents are fakes and phonies, then s/he will look elsewhere for confirmation. In many cases, this turning away from the family in the quest for authenticity is a risky enterprise and leads to experiments with sex, drugs, and various forms of escapism (dropping out, substituting media for direct experience) that can end in disaster and loss of valuable time in the process of life-development.

In extreme forms, this break from the family can lead to isolation when the teenager discovers that neither family nor peer group provides an adequate foundation for authentic existence. Many young American women try to solve their problems by having a child, with or without a partner in place. They hope, in this way, to compensate for losses and to make up for defeats.

When the quest for identity works within the American family, the result can be very positive and creative, indeed. Parent-child relationships take on the quality of friendships, and parents may find, later in life, that they can turn to their children for support and counsel. Both sides may realize that they can talk to one another in a real way, and they may discover that they have some common interests that they can pursue together. They may even travel together as companions; and they may write to one another in the spirit of mutual self-examination and exploration of the other.

I believe that I have had some of this experience with my mother, brother, and daughter (emphasis on *some*), though I never managed to penetrate my late father's resistant carapace of self. At the same time, I have written about some of these failures, thus transmuting them, in part, into kinds of successes. A failure on the home front, in America, is sometimes a success on the social and educational/creative side.

These are three of the assets-liabilities that American teachers take out to the world as part of their cultural baggage. Usually, they are convinced that these values, when well developed and well practiced, will serve everyone's interests. If they stay out in the world long enough, they may become somewhat skeptical about these precious preconceptions; if they are lucky, they will be able, as I've suggested, blending and merging the outgoing and returning self. I want to enumerate here the three most significant differences between American society and the more or less traditional societies in which I have lived and taught and learned.

(A) Cooperative Effort. Traditional societies, such as Turkey, Malaysia, India, and even Hong Kong, which, in some respects, is more traditional than the post-1949 PRC, put more emphasis on one's membership in a group than on one's identity and existence separate from the group. In my three years as a lecturer in the University of Hong Kong, an individual student rarely came to see me in my office to ask a question of a personal or academic nature. Students came in groups of two or three, usually before an essay assignment was due, and they would say, "*We* have a question; we don't understand." There may be many ways to interpret this behavior: custom, what I call cultural shyness, uncertainty about a foreigner's expectation, self-consciousness about individual competence in English, decorum (most of the students are women); but however it is construed, the social fact is that students function in a group.

This operates at all levels in the university. Students eagerly join associations that represent departments. Students present thank-you cards, signed by all members, at the end of a term. The cards appear mysteriously in one's "pigeon hole"; an individual member does not present them. I am not saying that students do not possess individual identity. This may or may not be the case. I am saying only that the expression of self (however we define it) takes place in a collective and often cooperative context. And when one does get to know an individual student "off campus," it usually needs to start in a group context before it can take another step. In my case, I continued to meet with a group of my American literature students (whom I called the "core" and who then took on the name for themselves).

The group ethic serves many positive functions. Among others, it establishes a standard of achievement to which everyone in the group aspires. Deviation from the perceived norm is not considered to be a virtue in this system. In the simplest of terms, one tries to fit in, not stand out. This system has limitations, to be sure. It leads to predictable work in many cases, and it encourages many forms of near-plagiarism. There is a thin line between "reference" and plagiarism that the Hong Kong students walk in an effort "to fit in." When one goes through a set of essays or exams, it's often as if one were listening to a univocal voice. At the same time, that voice is in key and comprehensible. In many ways, the American system reverses the priorities.

(B) Cultural continuity. Students in traditional societies assume that their teachers possess knowledge, if not wisdom, and hold correct, if not popular, opinions. In particular in Asia, teachers are "experts." I gave a lecture in Korea (1992) on "Henry James and the Web of Modernity: The Ends of Criticism in an Anglo-American Context." Although I had written a doctoral dissertation on Henry James and published a few articles from it. I did not, in typical American fashion, consider myself an "expert."

Even if I had considered myself an expert, I would not have introduced myself as one. In this case, I really didn't think that I was a James "specialist" (more acceptable American academic terminology), so I began by saying that I was not an expert, but someone who was familiar with James and always came back to his writing for renewed under-standing of the American experience.

At the end of the lecture a postgraduate student came up to the podium and said that he liked my talk very much but was confused because I had said that I wasn't an expert. He didn't know whether to trust my conclusions or not. To simplify matters and to make his evening more enjoyable and profitable, I told him that I was a "kind of expert," that my remark was a social gesture of politeness, that it was a gesture of civility in America (despite TV images of street violence).

He was pleased, of course, because I invoked an Asian standard of politeness to explain my mystifying behavior. He thanked me again for my lecture and said that he would doubtless make reference to it in something he was working on. He informed me, in leaving, that he was a "Henry Adams expert." My Korean colleague believed in cultural continuity. He believed that scholars transmit the accrued knowledge of the past without interposing their own points of view, though it must be added that a new generation of post-structuralist and post-modernist critics are calling these stereotypes of knowledge into question all over the world.

But even where my Korean colleague might have agreed that a scholar reinterprets the past, he probably would have said that such reinterpretations become definitive in turn, that one expert's views yield to another's. Opinions may change, but not the status of the scholar-expert. There is much to be said for and against this cultural-academic norm: it limits the field of opinion; it segregates scholars from one another if they are not in the same field; it makes postgraduate students and young scholars cautious about challenging their elders.

On the other hand, fields stay in a stable condition for a longer period of time, and those who follow take the carefully worked out conclusions of one generation very seriously. New streets and walls are added to the city of knowledge in traditional societies, whereas in America, to say nothing of Europe, Generation Y may be working in Old Town while

Generation X is building a new suburban, ex-urban, or extra-terrestrial community.

Traditional societies run the risk of preserving too many fossil records; post-traditional societies run the risk of breaking an organic evolutionary chain that links people through time and space. Hyper- and virtual reality (to say nothing of genetic engineering) may lead to new worlds, but these new worlds, if they do not bear significant relation to the old ones, can lead to ethical confusion and can make monsters of us all. Somehow, it won't do to be either a fossil or a monster.

(C) Membership in the family. Once I had socialized with the "core" somewhat, I got to know a few individual students, but when we met, we usually talked about their struggle to be themselves within a set of restrictions within the family, a framework they resented in some ways, but which they did not challenge. For some of these students, individuality would have to be expressed in a private and secret context or out of the colony.

In three years, only one student ever told me that s/he was in love with someone, that s/he hated a parent (for a while), that s/he wished to live alone. But even this person expected his/her mother to serve congee on examination mornings and believed that s/he was entitled to the largest inheritance as the first-born of a number of children. This student even wished in some ways, in certain moods, that the inhibiting parents would die, so long as an inheritance would make an affluent life in Hong Kong possible.

At the same time, these "death-wishes" were, I believe, the student's way of expressing a desire to have an independent existence, not true hatred of the parents. If given a chance for mutual understanding and clarification of life-differences, this student would have opted for conversation and dialogue, but such an option didn't exist in the present circumstance.

Having said this, it must be said that this student is, to the entire world, a dutiful son/daughter. Filial piety is in place. And it must be added that this person takes great comfort in the security of the family home away from which and out of which deep anxiety would be experienced – unless this person were building an addition to the family house through marriage, the reservoir of hope, renewal, and continuity in this rather surprisingly traditional society.

The sense of belonging cannot be overestimated as a social value, and the cost of denigrating its value can be very high. A close look at acts of social pathology in America almost always reveals patterns of childhood neglect and abandonment. It turns out that unhinged persons just weren't raised with proper hinges. The doors of self were off the jambs. My former Hong Kong student would like, often enough, to bust out of his/her house and to stand naked – self-revealed – on a beach in a world without inhibitions. America's legacy of self-expression might play better in this part of the world than it does in America itself near the end of the American Century – one of the themes of these essays.

As I suggested earlier, what's important now in world history is what we may be able to share. Writers and scholars have always participated in this process, but it needs to become a more general habit of mind for more people in the world. A good example is the fate of Thoreau's 1846 essay "Civil Disobedience": Tolstoy brought it to public attention in 1900; later, the young Indian lawyer Gandhi came upon it in South Africa and made use of it in his 1907 formulation of "The Ethics of Passive Resistance," which text had a profound impact a half-century later upon Dr. Martin Luther King Jr. (Frederick B. Tolles, *An American Primer*, ed. Daniel J. Boorstein, New York: A Mentor Book, 1968, pages 356–359).

Good ideas circulate and cross borders. There is no stopping them in the fullness of time. Gresham's Law does not operate in the world of ideas; though state-imposed opinion can dominate a culture's life long enough to lead to tragic ends. It seems now that it would be ill advised for me to try to adjudicate between my two sets of intellectual assets and liabilities. It is a subtle process that requires continuous assessment and evaluation. It may be sufficient, at this point, to say merely that the terms of voyage have been reversed in our time. If it was once clear that one should travel Port Out, Starboard Home (POSH), that one should, in effect, leave and return with one's fundamental social and cultural baggage in the same relative position, this is no longer the case. The imperial idea of unified Western states and cultures exerting singular influence in world affairs have been replaced by the notion of variety and difference, multiplicity and contrast.

At its best, this is a kind of liberation, an opportunity for individuals and societies to make their own amalgam of meaning, to make use of the world as a global resource. At its worst, this freeing up of identity makes each person, region, and country a lonely planet traveler. So, we need to travel and to cross borders; we need to recognize differences (a simultaneous awareness of who we are and who the other is); we need to talk, to exchange ideas; and, finally, we need to embrace the best way of doing things, no matter the point of origin. Starboard Out, Port Home.

Re-vision

As a child of the Second World War, I wanted to join the Navy and "see the world." Later, a fallen guru, who worked as a chef at my father's failed hotel in Far Rockaway, Twin Manor, read my palm and told me that I had a long lifeline. He sparked my interest in India and writing about India. I read Somerset Maugham's *The Razor's Edge* with great interest and wanted to write a book like it one day. Then, the motto of Amherst College, *Terras Irradient*, "Let us enlighten the world," raised the ante and pointed me in the direction of some kind of global exploration.

I took the first, almost fatal, step when I took a year off from college and served as a chauffeur and drinking companion for a sad, lonely, and wealthy uncle for a trip throughout the UK and Europe. We argued from Copenhagen to Britain and beyond to France, Portugal, Gibraltar, Casablanca, and other ports of call. This trip proved to be unsettling in a number ways, and in the end, I didn't feel as if I belonged anywhere wholly.

I did see enough of Europe in a positive sense, in the sense that I had hoped to see it through my imaginative projection in Fort Tyron Park and The Cloisters, to know that I would have to compose in part my identity in the future out of the culture and history of Europe. I never could be American again in a narrow sense. At the same time, the year with my late uncle had made Europe into an anxious object for me. My uncle and Europe were virtually synonymous terms in my mind for many years. In fact, I gave up chances to study in Scotland and England because of those associations.

It wasn't until twenty-five years later, when I was awarded a Fulbright to Turkey, that I began another kind of journey: a reversal of my family's history in some way. Where my grandfather had come to America to escape poverty and the pogroms, I would go to Asia Minor in a quest of a measure of antiquity to give some balance and ballast to the lack of cohesion in American life after the 1960s, an America torn by racial, ethnic, and gender conflicts, an America that often preferred the fantasies of Hollywood movies and television sit-coms to the rhythms of everyday life — in part because we didn't have those rhythms.

As the journey continued, its surface meaning, or the meaning of its surface, shifted for me. But I think I always have been looking for a home away from home – a symbolic home, a universal home, yet a home rooted in history. When my daughter and my grandson moved to Israel four years ago, I entered another phase of my reversal of history. The Old World that my grandfather had fled and the even Older World of the Old Testament that he had not been able to share with me because we didn't speak the same language (he, Yiddish, I, English) now became for me a version of a New World. I was now, with my daughter and her family, "out of the Diaspora," but I wasn't out of its contradictions for me.

I have explored these tragi-comic contradictions in a series of nine short stories that I have written over the past five years, and I make use of my travels in my stories. The Seine, Danube, Bosporous, and Jordan flow through them. If I had not traveled out, I would have remained an unexcavated site of layered identity; if I had not returned home to share my experiences in various ways with generations of students, I would have hoarded my treasure and failed to prepare them, to the extent that America will allow them to prepare, for a life of global diversity and cooperation: a dream, of course; a possible reality? It's still too soon to know.

In expanding my world, I gave up the possibility of a fixed identity. In testing the limits of what R.D. Laing calls ontological security, I never was certain when I returned from an overseas experience to what extent I belonged in America. At the same time, my house and circle of friends became more important to me as a "stay against confusion" in the words of the American poet Robert Frost. I never would become a Wagner, so to speak, and try to make my house into a fortress; but each voyage out made me more of a gardener when I returned.

Travel made me long to belong somewhere, at least for certain periods of time, and where I lived, in fact, was a good place to begin. If I was away in late spring or early summer, I always missed the blossoming of *my* crimson-centered white peonies and the scent of *my* lavender lilac bush. The more I became an international man; the more I wanted to cultivate my little lot of land. In thinking of leaving again, I always feel sad that I may not see my English ivy show new growth next year. It is no wonder that the British became famous for their small gardens. They were an outgrowth of life in the colonies and a need for roots.

CHAPTER NINE

HOMAGE TO BROWARD COUNTY: THE END OF THE LITTORAL

I have lived with South Florida in my bones, like Eliot's sense of literary history, since 1943 when my mother, brother, and I first took the Seaboard Express to Miami Beach, so my relation to Florida over the years serves as a timeline embedded with millions of bits of data. I start with broken tiles, jagged and obdurate, and try to shape a mosaic pattern. What shall I look at first? I think of Frost's "The Figure a Poem Makes" and his logic of composition: "Like a piece of ice on a hot stove the poem must ride on its own melting." Where shall I begin?

Out of all possible "Floridiana," to give a name to the matter of Florida that might serve as well as the name of a condominium complex or shopping mall, I am driven to choose a photo of my grandson Tyler, age three, as my point of departure. Tyler represents the ending and possible renewal of my "Histoire de Florida," as the late Robert Creeley calls his poetic investigation into Florida in which he speculates, "Perhaps the whole place is a giant pier out/into nothing, or into all that is other, all else."

It is in relation to Tyler, if only in my mind, that I must decide if I would wish for him to live one day in the future, however occasionally, in my parents' condominium. The Cascades on Northwest 50th Street in Lauderhill just to the south of Veterans Park and west of Flakowitz's Delicatessen. In reviewing my life in relation to my history in and of Florida, I feel that I must decide, if only as a matter of literary archeology, if I would wish him to become a lodger, in some fashion, in my parents' version of what Stephen Crane surely would have called Hotel de Dream if he had lived to write a book about domestic life of exilic New Yorkers in Florida.

In the end – or does it represent the possibility for a new beginning? – the culmination of my history of Florida will come down to a question of inheritance. Will I want to keep my half-share of a condominium that I am destined to inherit, more or less within the next few decades, so that I can then, in the fullness of time, pass it on to Tyler?

This will be a difficult decision for many reasons, including the need to separate language from facts, symbols from landscape. From the time of Ponce de Leon through Flagler to the present, Florida has been a collection point for exotic naming. The language of dreams wafts through the air along with the scent of banyan and cypress, yellow tab, trumpet honeysuckle, flame-of-the-woods *(Ixora)*, and hibiscus, so it is sometimes difficult to know where you are until you see a sign that says "Jap cars only" or "Ashes Shipped North," until you look hard and accept what you see.

The names themselves take you away to other places. *Florida's Fabulous Flowers* says: "The name of *Ixora* comes from Ishwara, one of the many names for the Hindu god, Shiva. along India's Malabar Coast, the flowers of certain *Ixora* species are used as temple offerings." In driving to Lauderdale-by-the-Sea, the Broward County beach closest to my parents' condo, about ten miles away, a beach they never have sat or walked on, I am carried away by names. I think of India, a country I have visited three times, particularly of a village in the State of Orissa on the Bay of Bengal, Gopalpur-on-Sea, near Berhampur University, where I have friends who wish me to come back one day.

Crossing Florida's Turnpike and I-95, I try, if only as an imaginative game to get through the traffic and the homeless hawkers of the *Sun Sentinel,* to see myself in retirement, whatever that may mean to a writer after his life as a university teacher is over, living in *either* Lauderhill, the site of my parents' condo, *or* Gopalpur-by-Sea, where I could gather sweet coconuts on the beach, watch daily rituals unfold, and get to know, over time, most of the villagers who would be aware of my presence. Gopalpur calls me back to something like Kipling's "old Moulmein Pagoda."

I am haunted by a version of a decades-old tension between domestic and overseas possibilities for living and working: Buffalo and Turkey; Buffalo and Malaysia; Buffalo and Hong Kong; Buffalo and elsewhere, home and away. Why did I leave? Why did I return? To sell or not to sell? – That will be the question.

I return to the photo of Tyler. Everything that matters is contained there. He stands a little stiffly, puffed up for the instamatic photo-session, within the shadow of a banyan tree whose branches arch toward my parents' condo-unit on one side and a modest-size lake on the other. He is the only person in view. He wears a wee tee-shirt, swimming trunks, and sandals, a regular vacationer. He clutches a mysterious object. A duck sits on the slightly mounded edge of the lake. The lake is streaked with sunlight reflected off the white-faced units directly opposite my parents' place. These units, with their walkways and enclosed screen porches, remind me of the Scoffield barracks in *From Here to Eternity* and my own quarters at Camp Belvoir, Virginia, in 1959, where I observed, unknowingly, the first stirrings of the Vietnam war when unidentified Asian soldiers carried bags of rice to nameless barracks.

Just before taking the photograph, Tyler said, "I like that duck, I want him." I understood his impulse to possess living nature. I thought also that he felt a little lonely standing out there in the midst of what must have seemed like gigantic buildings without anyone but his grandfather in sight. He's a friendly little fellow, with a tropism for energy and motion, and he was doubtless eager to have a playmate. The duck would do for the moment. What does this photo mean to me? Is this the place where I want to end up? Is this the Floridian enclave that I wish Tyler to inherit one day? How did I get here? What does Florida – particularly the postage stamp corner of Broward County – mean to me?

In order to answer this question (to the sea or not to the sea?), I must go back to the beginning of my time in Florida. As I've said, I first went to Miami Beach with my mother and brother by train in 1943. My father was too busy working and making money during the boom years, for the garment business, of the Second World War, to go with us. It was a little embarrassing to me that my father wasn't serving his country, so it was just as well, for this and other reasons, that he wasn't traveling with us. Miami Beach was the destination for people like my parents, New York City Jews, children of immigrants, for whom a trip to Miami Beach in the winter was a sign of success, the social equivalent of a big Bar Mitzvah at one of Manhattan's better hotels (in my case, the Dorset), much as it is for Russian Jewish immigrants today who, after a decade or two, are beginning to make it in America. The Dorset is now an archeological site, a footprint under the expanded Museum of Modern Art (MoMA).

A trip to Florida in 1943 was also a patriotic exercise and a lesson in American history – its energy, sense of mission, giantism. Men and women of the armed forces briskly criss-crossed the then-polished marble floors of Pennsylvania Station under the glass and steel–enclosed platforms on furlough or en route to one form or other of the war. Far from communicating fear or anxiety, their young adult faces and starched uniforms expressed pride and self-assurance. They believed in their bones that they were defending and fighting for the greatest country in the world at the height of its power in the American Century; history had swept them up to defeat Hitler, Hirohito, and Mussolini; every quick step and stride conveyed clarity of identity and purpose. I wanted the war to last until I would be old enough to fight in it.

Although I was not very self-aware about Jewish identity then and knew nothing about the death-camps, I was proud nonetheless that so many Americans who weren't Jewish were going off to war to fight the murderous Nazis and the "sneaky" Japanese who had made my mother cry on December 7, 1941, when our beloved FDR announced the "day that will live in infamy." Standing in Penn Station with my mother and brother, my mother's steamer trunk, a relic of nineteenth-century baggage, being wheeled to the platform by a smiling and deferential red-cap (tips and stereotypes were big in those days), I felt that our family belonged in, and was accepted by, America. I did not know then that our trip to Florida, the first of many, was a step toward the displacement of my parents' generation of Jews from New York, another stage of the historic diaspora, a distant relative of 1492, the expulsion from Spain.

We were on the move, and it seemed to be in the right direction. At the same time, there was something mysterious and a little frightening about the world beyond New York (my brother hadn't yet crossed the Hudson River to go to The University of Wisconsin at Madison in 1949). As I wrote in a poem some years ago when I still wrote poetry, "Florida was the end of the wilderness." As much as I believed that the war effort had made our family definitively American (my grandfather still spoke Yiddish, after all), I still wasn't quite sure about the rest of America. Would we be accepted everywhere? Would real Floridians look at me and know that three of my father's brothers, even though they were left wing, were ready to die in a war against Fascism? In fact, one was wounded in the landing at Normandy.

It was comforting, after a night in a compartment or Pullman sleeper, to see the sun break over orange groves, causeways, and the pastel facades of South Beach. We were, sort of, home. Miami Beach seemed to be, magically, a tropical suburb of New York.

We made several trips to Miami Beach during the war years and immediately afterward, the high point of my father's business life, before he went bust, bankrupt and belly-up, but these trips remain as one in my mind, a tableau as fixed as the carved coconuts that still hold talismanic power for me: palm trees and Art Deco facades illuminated by neon and multicolored floodlights; a lime and lemon-yellow sea caressing my young and somewhat guilty body; the swelling breasts of young women who seemed eager to display their emerging bodies, unembarrassed by the off-and-on bulge in my bathing suit; my brother and I, standing in a pugilistic pose in front of a bowed royal palm. It was, largely, a world of pleasure, perhaps the only one I would know in an uncomplicated way.

But that world didn't last. My father's life was consumed with bankruptcy and a loss of confidence and pride; my uncle Sam, our tribal leader and mogul, who lived in Miami Beach after the war, got ripped off by the Mafia, lost his financial interest in the Dream Bar, a swanky place that had become a kind of temporary home for him, and began three decades of exilic traveling with which I would catch up ten years later — both the traveling and something like the exile. I was to learn later that the bonds between "exiles," if only as an imagined state of mind, can be stronger, if impermanent, than those between ones many friends at home.

Florida disappeared during my high school, college, and graduate years. It returned only as a sense-memory when I went on a honeymoon to Jamaica in 1963 and smelled an ambrosial mixture of coconut oil, Caribbean sea, pungent tropical vegetation, and perfume (my child bride's Givenchy, a memory of my mother's Tabu) as a cocktail pianist played a medley of Cole Porter songs, "Begin the Beguine," and Helen O'Connell's rendition of "Green Eyes." Those songs still resonate. Good popular music contains the all of the essential truths.

I didn't go back to Florida until the early 1970s when my parents left New York to retire in, first, Port St. Lucie, west of the Indian River where my mother prudently had bought a small house, with disciplined savings from a modest job (out of reach of my father), in anticipation of my father's decline and fall. I say retire, but it was more like expire, more like Club Dread than Club Med, or so it felt to me.

Although I silently had fought with my father since birth, I was caught off guard by my feelings of loss of home-as-place when I first went to visit them in 1970. These feelings are revealed in this poem:

> Today, the calm at the end of the night
> Is shadowed with Malls and Mobile Camps.
> Airstream caravans are cemented to the sand,
> And white stone picnic tables, funeral
> Slabs, wait for those who are waiting
> For a child, grandchild, or old friend.
> Death sits at the side of the road making its bid in a cheap
> price war.

I was deeply saddened, if not devastated, by the loss of New York, the city that held all my father's history, most of my mother's, most of mine. My mother's childhood in central Pennsylvania and Pembroke, Ontario, my summer camp in Kent, Connecticut – everything out of New York was *elsewhere*.

The ex-poet writes in another poem:

> A marriage lies behind me now,
> A broken skiff, sanded over
> On this sliding spit of Florida coast
> My parents call home
> Which is not my home,
> Which I dutifully visit once a year
> Because death will come soon
> And I fear the aftermath of guilt.
> Here at Port St. Lucie, crippled brakemen
> On compensation and postal clerks, pensioned,

Wait for the morning mail and their children.
I think of the girl from Cumberland Island.
I should have gone with her across the river.

I made those early trips with reluctance, unwilling to acknowledge the permanence of my parents' move, though I recognized the necessity, if not the wisdom, of their flight from New York. Even as I understood that my father could hide his failure more easily in Florida than New York (he didn't run into cronies who knew about his tax case), his being in Florida itself represented failure to me; and his limitations, as I felt them, were exaggerated in Florida. He was afraid of nature and his movie version of "wild Indians." He had cut down in his yard the one young Royal Poinciana tree because he thought he might bump into it, and he believed that the Seminoles, who had yet to sign a definitive treaty with the U.S. government, might cross Lake Okeechobee and attack. My father's fantasies were comic, of course, but they also were oppressive and embarrassing.

In some ways, he became more threatening to me in Florida than he had been in New York. It became less easy to escape his presence in Florida when I visited than it had been in New York, where I could, after all, just step outside their apartment house into the vortex of the city and lose myself, disappear. In Florida, to escape this strange man who was all too present as my father, I had to drive to get away; and that meant making him aware of my desire to flee. "Stop driving the ass out of my car," he would say sometimes, displacing the issue. In time, I would turn to Alamo car rental, but that didn't conceal my "wandering," as my father called it. It just annoyed him a little less.

If the loss of New York pained me, it allowed me to explore my battle with my father, our New York Jewish version of the war of the Titans, to bring some clarity to a struggle that had been surfacing in my life for many years. I wrote a short story and a fictional memoir in 1974 that took a parricidal, if also antic, view of my father. If visiting my parents during the first years of their exile from New York was difficult because I had to face at once a loss of home and my father's outsize presence, I was able to make something out of the difficulty: poems, a story, and, finally, a book – that sacred and profane academic object which I needed to affirm my existence and to secure academic tenure, *Forgive the Father: A Memoir of Changing Generations.*

Florida was becoming increasingly and ironically more of an enclave for family reflection and rumination than New York had been. If New York had been a maelstrom, Florida was a small lake. If New York had been a jungle, Florida was just what it was where my parents lived after they left Port St. Lucie (because my father claimed that my mother was "burying him" there): a confined and landscaped condominium. First, at Cypress Tree, the condominium where they lived for ten years; then, five miles north on University Avenue in Lauderhill, The Cascades, where there is no waterfall. Though they were uprooted in Florida, the roots were visible in a way that they never had been before. More and more, each visit made clear that I was entering – anxiously, longingly? – a world of pure family relations.

As years passed, annual visits (verging on pilgrimages now) accrued, and frequent-flyer mileage piled up. I found, in my thinking and writing, that I was becoming preoccupied with the theme of home – with the loss of our original one in New York and what would be my parents' last home, their resting place in Florida. This theme became particularly pressing and poignant when my parents informed me that they would be buried in Florida in the Star of David Memorial Gardens in Tamarac, a few miles from where they lived.

To avoid any confusion about this, my mother, who tends to be frank, sent me a receipt of the transaction. As I recall, an invitation came with it as well, to buy a plot for myself ... at a discount. I was appalled by the whole business and asked my father if he didn't really want to be buried in New York, where he had lived all his life. "What?! And be shipped North like an orange?" he replied. He had a point, though at the time I was sure that I would prefer to take my place, when the time came, in the Jewish Cemetery in Cheektowaga, New York, which lies, in a lesser suburb of Buffalo, next to an expressway on one side and a fast-food restaurant on the other. Now I am less sure.

My confusions and ambivalences emerged in a novel, I'd written mainly between 1981 and 1983, *Broadway Serenade*, where the hero, who is described as a *"luftmench* in synthetics,"* has a vision of himself flying on Dacron wings over Manhattan in order to purchase a panoramic view of his parents' trek North to Washington Heights. It was clear, by the time I had finished the novel in first draft and rewritten it in different parts of the world where I was teaching over the next decade (Turkey, Malaysia, Hong Kong), that it never would be easy for me to abandon the site of my parents' life and, ultimately, death. If it was clear in 1970 that New York was their home, it was almost as clear by 1990, when they celebrated their sixtieth anniversary, that Florida was now their second home.

And, to some extent, I realize now that, beneath my resistance to the idea of ever retiring to my parents' condo, beneath my sense of social alienation (an unanchored wanderer in a world of yachts, a thinking reed afloat in a sea of bikinis, an authentic neurotic among happy campers), I had begun to imagine myself spending some part of each year at some point in the future in The Cascades. During recent visits, I have found myself redesigning my parents' condo, looking at flowers and trees more carefully, sitting at a certain window – writing.

Sadly, disturbingly, this turn of my psyche has been made possible, just that, by my father's somewhat mysterious and undiagnosed withdrawal over the past decade. Though he does not suffer from Alzheimer's disease or more than slight and occasional dementia, he has stepped away from the world. He sleeps eighteen hours a day, much of the time slumped over in an easy chair in which he no longer reads the *Wall Street Journal* or studies, almost Talmudically, stock reports; and, though he will answer a question about his past if I ask one, he will not sustain a conversation.

My father, who always bullied me with his unchecked ego, has now disappeared into a world about which he refuses to talk. If I try to get him to share his problem with me, he tells me to "get the hell out of here." If I try to probe his inner state, he threatens to take pills, nervously retreats, and tells me to leave him alone. I now accept this, though it means that we never shall have that talk of Truth and Reconciliation; and, in accepting this, it has become easier for me to visit my mother, for my father is no longer powerfully present. His life is largely in the hands of a Caribbean day-nurse who ministers to his needs while my mother and I chat about some of the pleasures of the earlier years in New York City. We sometimes thought it would be best if they ran off together to Jamaica, but that didn't happen.

On my last visit, the time of the photo, I walked with Tyler every morning around the condo's lake through a cypress grove to the pool; and every evening I took him to Veterans Park where the moon, suspended in a net of Spanish moss that laced the weeping banyan, hung like an infinitely slow pitch above the Little League field. I compared these two mini-worlds and wondered if they could be reconciled so that it would make some sense to think about living in the condo and then passing it on to Tyler.

I wondered if I ever would be able to sell, to set sail for Gopalpur-on-Sea, to begin a new life, a life consciously detached from my past – insofar as one can do that by walking away from physical and environmental actualities, from a theater or museum of memory. Would I be capable, finally, of shifting my soul from an ambivalent, but known past to an unwritten, but uncertain, future?

Tyler and I walked, hand in hand, in a largely empty and silent world in the early morning. Few of the residents go to the pool before noon. If they are up, they are likely to be catering to the needs of an infirm spouse or visiting one of many doctors. My parents never lie out in the sun, though they left New York, in part, because they found it too cold. The Fit Trail – one of the developer's gimmicks or fantasies – is unused; and the Shuffleboard court is largely grown over.

There is some activity in the clubhouse – the social hub of all condos – in the evenings: cards and bingo, an occasional broken-down singer or comic who no longer can be booked into a hotel; but my parents don't attend. Although my father would never admit it, even at those times when he was capable of some insight, the clubhouse always meant "less than New York" to him, once he was out of it.

For reasons that I never understood, my father had lived as an unaffiliated man all his life. He wasn't about to take up gin rummy as an antidote to loneliness in his old age at a time when he had developed cataracts. Sex and the stock market had been his connection to the world in his vigorous period. With the waning of desire and the shift from volatile stocks to long, stable bonds, he had become a one-man Diaspora without a sense of history. Sometimes, I thought of saying this in the hope of lending some scope to his exilic tendencies, but he would have told me to "tell it to the Marines", even if he hadn't served.

But even the couples who play gin rummy and plan trips to Disney World, who gossip by the pool in the warm weather, live essentially for a world elsewhere, for the time when their children and grandchildren will visit during the winter holidays and spring break, for it is only then that they feel as if they really belong to a larger world. Only when the children and grandchildren come do they look animated. Only then does the condo make sense as an index of family history, of success in America. Why, then, did they come? Perhaps the impulse to flee the perceived growing violence of New York, perhaps the need to have some visible reward for a life of work other than a bank account, which one doesn't, after all, show around. Why do many, if not most, people go somewhere else after a life of work? As in illness, some prefer to be alone when weakened.

Still, the place has a kind of beauty in the early morning. Red bottlebrush trees fleck the sky, and birds seem to be at their ease: a hawk nesting here, a heron there. The grounds are well tended at The Cascades, and one can imagine that, in time, the place may become a kind of bird sanctuary, if over-development of the larger environment doesn't destroy surviving species. I had a vision the morning of the photo: that one day, in Tyler's maturity, The Cascades might return to Florida's original state, with sawgrass and hummock replacing blacktop and strip-mall; that Ponce de Leon's dream of a beginning would replace a site of endings that Florida largely had turned into; but there are many problems in this once potential paradise, including a sick palm that one of the groundskeepers, a Cuban immigrant who has a nose for decay, told me about. I wondered if this irremediably sick tree was an augury or symbol.

It would seem likely that it's too late for me, the likes of me, to live with any measure of satisfaction and harmony in the kind of Florida that I remembered from childhood when the Everglades was still real wilderness and fish plashed in the New River, but there are moments, when I watch Tyler play in Veterans Park, on the evenings of the spring solstice for instance, that this landscape, even country, might be redeemed. Befriended by Kareem, a Jamaican-American, who let him ride his bike, and Hermilene, a Filipina girl, who lifted him onto the jungle-gym, Tyler began to think of the world around The Cascades as a less lonely world, a world with people and life in it. Watching Little League with one eye and Tyler with the other, watching the now grown children of poor Southern whites cheer on African-American kids who were teammates of their children, I began to think, on these solstice evenings, that America might overcome its historic sin and potentially fatal self-inflicted wound.

It was possible, on these evenings, to think that, if the worlds of The Cascades and Veterans Park were to merge in time, if Flakowitz's walls were to come down, like Berlin's,

America might become a dream come true, might become a place in which homage to the past would not preclude growth and change. It became possible "for a transitory enchanted moment," as the narrator says at the end of *The Great Gatsby*, to think that a choice to keep the condo for myself, for my heir and Kaddish, Tyler, might become something other than a pious and regressive attachment to the past, a subtropical museum of family history in which displacement, social isolation, dying, and death were delivered with the *Sun Sentinel*.

And I could sustain these feelings at the beach, particularly within the confines of Hugh Taylor Birch State Recreation Area, at the intersection in Ft. Lauderdale of Sunrise Boulevard and A-I, where, within fewer than 200 acres, wading birds still can be seen in a hummock-enclosed lagoon, and a remnant of mangroves provides a habitat, however limited, for several species of herons and other shoreline animals.

Standing in the shade and quiet of this tropical hardwood forest with Tyler, waiting for the appearance of a rare tortoise, I believe that it may be possible for us, for him, to step back into a meaningful past if we pick our time and spots carefully, if the State of Florida continues, at least here and there, to pursue a vigorous policy of conservation. It doesn't take too much protection in Florida for an area, even a postage stamp of one, to become a viable natural biosphere.

In this enclave, on a given day, I imagine saying farewell forever to Buffalo, my university work habitat of thirty years, when the time comes, despite the touristic snobbery of some friends who think only in terms of Tuscany, Provence, Greek Islands, and Caribbean. I imagine, watching Tyler watch a gliding hawk, a departure that would be an arrival, as well, an end that would be a true beginning in several senses.

I imagine a departure from Buffalo and a resettlement (or should I say *restetl*ment?) in Florida, my parents' second home for three decades, particularly when Tyler and I emerge from the tunnel that goes under A-IA and connects the park to the sea and see in front of us the lime and canary green currents of the Gulf Stream running through the grayer and bluer bands of the Atlantic.

There, on the beach in Ft. Lauderdale, condos to the north, tourist hotels to the south, with their day-long Happy Hours and wet tee-shirt contests, there, surrounded by thong-taut and curve-sculpted young women, watching Tyler's face illumined by the bright sea, I imagine letting go of two layers of the past, New York and Buffalo, a return to the deepest layers of the past that would be, at the same time, a fresh start of sorts. One couldn't beat the rap completely, but there might be moments of reprieve.

From an early age, water, lake, and sea had meant release and freedom to me. I didn't own the archetype, but it felt real and always had worked for me. If I didn't judge summers anymore by the number of ponds, rivers, and seas in which I had swum, I still responded happily to the lift of the waves and the thrill of the horizon lines with nameless freighters and ocean liners sailing into unknown waters. My mother accused me now and then of never being happy, but she wasn't completely right. There were moments near and in the sea, which granted a certain happiness; but how can one tell one's mother that one's emotional salvation is measured in moments?

But even if returning to Florida, for part, if not all, of the year, the first step toward oblivion for many "snow birds," might be a form of museology for me, it might be just what the doctor ordered, if not a general cure, a way of overcoming the loneliness of dislocation and provincial exile. I could read all the obituaries in the *Buffalo News* for thirty years and never comprehend, at depth, the lives that had been lived there. In this corner of Florida, I understood everything; and, when I understood too much, I could ogle the lithe volleyball fans in bikinis at the Iguana Beach Bar. A museum, with some release, might keep me afloat.

The Wolf family may have run its course, in many ways, in America in the twentieth century from "tailor to Tyler," as I was becoming fond of saying; but it hadn't quite disappeared.

Beginning in poverty and anonymity in the first decade of the century, my parents created space in that crowded world for their children, who, if they hadn't achieved fame, had been able, at least, to express themselves, to offer bread and the risk of freedom to their children. Their corner of the condo, their place, was the physical embodiment of the heroism of the Jewish middle class (of all caring parenthood), of the struggle for decency (with all of its exclusions and prohibitions). It would not be easy for me, when the time came, to force a sale, call the auctioneer, and hand over keys to a stranger. In decency, attention must be paid to the struggle of the elders. My father had once summarized his early life on the Lower East Side to me in a letter:

> "It was a struggle in 1917, when the war was on. We had to wait in line to get coal. Food was scarce. Ice in the summer time. I had to go to the East River to get a piece of ice for 10 cents and bring it home in a hand-made wagon. Once kids who wanted to steal my ice and wagon attacked me, and they beat me black and blue, but I wouldn't let go of my wagon. I remember my father had a little place on Bayard Street near Chinatown. He used to take old pants and dip them in kerosene and then cut out the new parts of the pants and make knee pants for boys. We then had to put them on a wagon and take them to Mulberry Street and sell them to the people living there. My father used to cry out loud, "Rubba, buno, no cottuna!" (Meaning "all wool, no cotton"). This was a hard way to make a living, and I went with him a lot of times."

The earliest part of this story – my grandfather Jacob Wolf's escape from the Czar's army – and its middle section – mercantile success from the middle 1920s to the middle 1950s, despite the Depression – were as familiar as my father's childhood to his generation of New York Jews. But the ending of the story wasn't clear as yet, and I had become part of it. Friends might say, "Sell, walk away from it, you'll end up like them," but they could not hear the plain music of my father's soul.

He and I had fought for more than half a century, but I no more could hand over easily the keys of their condo, with their objects and memorabilia – so common, so predictable – than I could tear up my father's letter. How could one walk away and not make a votive offering by accepting a sacred gift? At the same time, it was quite possible that I could do more in time, if I didn't sell, than muse without a muse among the ruins or shards of memory in the pool (Olympic-size, to be sure).

And it was hard to imagine Tyler living there in the socially and racially unified world that I was pretty sure he would want for himself one day. He might play on a given spring night with, and as part of, children of the rainbow coalition, but there were hidden and angry worlds of African-Americans and Hispanics less than a mile from The Cascades: fenced-off enclaves where people of color lived somewhat fearfully. They might not accept him.

"Whatever," as we say about all our impasses these days. My ambivalences might be eternal and unresolvable, but his psyche and life were another matter. It was risky to try to look into the crystal ball of his life. He held his own life in his hands; at least it was wise to think of him in those terms, as I hadn't succeeded in doing for his mother upon whom I was determined, usually, to try to impose my social ambitions and intellectual categories – if not domineering will in the style of my father.

If all my thinking and writing ended in some version of home and away, the only story I ever could think of, it needn't mean that Tyler need be freighted with a comparable load of self-consciousness. My grandfather had hawked "old clothes," a street cry I heard in my old Washington Heights neighborhood once or twice in my youth when vendors, knife grinders, and tinkers still made the rounds of the city; my father had carried a garment bag; I had borne the burden of memory, if not as a chalice, at least as a Sabbath kiddush cup; Tyler could find his own goblet to hold and cherish.

My writing had been, in its way, a version of the Sabbath prayer, without my ever knowing or thinking about it: a celebration of origins, a lament for flight and departure; a narrative of beginnings and endings, at once eulogy and elegy, humor and pathos, from Ellis Island to "Islandia," Lithuania to littoral. It would be wrong to impose this story upon Tyler in any literal fashion. I had to keep separate what was symbolic for me from what was only literal: real ducks in a real pond as he looked at his grandfather take a photo of him in the place where his great-grandparents, those ancient people, lived.

Tyler had not heard the cries of the wandering vendors, an aural remnant of Eastern Europe, a voice of need that allowed me to enter my father's echo chamber and there hear with him the cry of his father. Tyler would be free to see and hear the world freshly, even in Broward County. He could discover Florida for himself, its earlier history, even the honorable tenure as Governor of Napoleon Bonaparte Broward himself. He need not get caught up in the web of Jewish-American history, the world of his grandparents, and carry the burden of their displacement, their sense of Florida, however comfortable, as being a place "that is other."

Tyler would not have to feel himself always as an outsider to the older life of Ft. Lauderdale, as an alien of sorts at the counter of The Chemist Shop on Las Olas, itself forced to move now as rents escalate, where native Floridians talk about deep-sea fishing and of a time when the New River was "clear as gin." Even if many of these Floridians were as much Johnny-come-latelies as my parents, they had been able, as WASPS (there is no more exact way to say this), to fit into the older mode and *modus vivendi*. Even if they did not belong in a historical sense, they belonged in a cultural one. They defined the outlines of success. I couldn't be indifferent to them, but

Tyler could, and through him a new relation to Florida could be forged – one that included the past but went beyond it.

I had hoped that I would recall, in the process of writing this mosaic-in-progress, that I would remember what Tyler holds in his delicate and eager hands (I like to think that everything he does makes an impression on me; but it doesn't). Or maybe he carried or picked up something that I never saw. Whatever it is, it is, at least now, a mysterious object; and it is perhaps best that it is and remains so, for it serves as a reminder that his life is his own. He holds his own life in his hands. Whatever he actually is holding, it is his life that I must think of him as pressing close together.

So, will it make sense to try to Begin the Beguine again, or should I listen to a trusted poet friend, who has heard all the legends and lore, when the time comes, and sell? Should I walk away from the plot of the past? I don't know. I know only that the scales of my life feel equally weighted. Resolution feels like distortion, betrayal. It may be that I can do no better than to imagine keeping the condo as a site of memory, which I shall visit so long as I can afford to do so. I may not be able to do what a therapist suggested to me in Hong Kong: buy a bouquet of flowers, go to the Peak, lay them upon a spot that I mark as a symbolic burial site, and then say farewell. I balked at the idea then and I do now.

Among the documentary tiles that I gathered for this essay is a postcard, "Shells of Florida." When I bought it at Mack's Grove in Lauderdale-by-the-Sea, now for sale, I knew I wouldn't send it. I felt it might contain some information that would be useful to me: a list of "the many shells that you can find on a Florida beach," including the "margin shell," a closed and oval shape, not unlike the shape of Tyler's hands as he holds who knows what.

This is one of the literal things that one can find on the Florida littoral; it's also a symbol for me of the way we live our lives, our deepest thoughts concealed from view, our own past buried beneath the sand of consciousness: life at the margin, inner and outer, as we look for all the world like ordinary people leading ordinary lives; and perhaps that is just what ordinary lives are. When I asked a Norwegian gentleman at the Sandy Shoes Cafe and Iguana Beach Bar – now for sale — to take a photo of Tyler and me, he probably only saw a Henry Moore archetype of grandfather and grandson. Other worlds were hidden.

Re-vision

A great deal has changed, or perhaps I should say, "vanished" or "disappeared," since I wrote this essay, but the essentials remain the same and, if anything, have deepened. Hurricane Wilma uprooted and blew away the banyan tree in front of my parents' condominium; the Fit-Trail, never used, is splintered and hidden by growth; the Clubhouse is empty; most of the generation of New Yorkers who came to Florida between 1960 and 1980 have died, and the population of the condominiums is largely Hispanic and international. More deeply, for me, my father died in 1998, a few years after the essay was written, and Tyler now lives in Israel in a village on a hill overlooking the Sea of Galilee (Kinneret).

I no longer feel the strains of anger and resentment towards my father that I felt when I wrote the memoir. Time and mourning, grief and understanding, bring out reconciliation. One ages; one becomes more like one's parent of the same gender; and, unless one is quite masochistic, one comes to accept the parent in oneself and thus the parent.

Tyler now lives in a Jewish world more authentic than anything Florida could have been for him. Indeed, his Jewish world is more authentic than the one my grandfather Wolf lived in New York City where he was, too, always an exile of sorts. In a way that I never could have imagined or predicted, Tyler is now positioned to be more instructive about the Jewish world, its rituals, its ancient language, than ever my grandfather was able to be.

I dedicated my novel, *Broadway Serenade*, to Tyler in 1996: "To my grandson, Tyler, whose great-great-grandfather, Jacob Wolf, came to America as a penniless tailor in the first decade of the 20th Century – may he come to understand the journey and fulfill its promise." If I had thought that the progress was from "tailor" to "Tyler," I now see that it has been from "tailor" to "Ty*lor*," the Israeli pronunciation of his name now. In a reversal of history and identity, my grandson has become my grandfather's ancestor – or something like that.

But the fundamental themes have remained the same – the quest for identity and belonging, the balance of home and away, the leitmotif (but not "lite") of something like displacement and "exile" as underlying constituents of identity. If once I had thought that "Exile" put one at the margin and edge of the humanity community, I now see that one becomes, in however modest a fashion, especially if one travels and goes out into the world, an exile among exiles. And it is precisely this shared identity, " of "not belonging wholly," like the expats of Hong Kong, or the Wagners of Buffalo, that allows one to feel part of a symbolic community, as I felt briefly part of the universal "moan" in Calcutta.

In the concluding letter in my *A Version of Home: Letters from the World*, I write about a group of Indian students whom I say I shall remember as "an as yet unobservable constellation of stars," a provisionally real community that shall become symbolic for me in the moment of my departure. The Cascades, to which I still return to see my aging, but bright-eyed and clear-headed, mother will not become the kind of community that I fancifully imagined that it might become. Only the names of the luxury hotels and condominiums have utopian connotations.

It sometimes turns out that our futures turn out to be versions of the past. The future often lies hidden in the folds of the shawl of the past with enshrouded implications that will come to the light of day only at a much later date, usually the time of writing about the past.

CHAPTER TEN

THE NEW SOUTH AFRICA:
JOURNEY TOWARD DIGNITY

No one person, certainly no non–South African, can claim to make a definitive statement about the great transformation from the apartheid era to the "new South Africa" unless that person is former President Nelson Mandela, the "Black Pimpernel." And I pay homage to him, in my title, "Journey toward Dignity," an echo of his autobiography, *Long Walk to Freedom* (1994). But I lived and taught for the better part of a year in Bloemfontein, in the Free State – heart, when it had one, of the old Boer Republic – so I have some hope that I may find some diamonds of truth in the mines of my experience.

I want as much as possible to avoid abstraction. I want to state what I take to be some self-evident principles of human dignity and to illustrate these principles with reference to other people and to myself as observer and participant. In an age that has embraced relativism with a lover's passion, we need to resist the temptation to court the abyss of non-meaning at every turn. It is all too easy in a century characterized by enormity, genocide, and what the German government itself refers to as the "topography of terror," to displace the faces of humanity with faceless language as an act of denial.

If, then, even one person cannot live with dignity, if the actual conditions of one person's life prevent that person from living humanly, then we know (and it may be all we need to know) that that community is endangered. South Africa's Truth and Reconciliation Commission (TRC) served the nation and the world by letting the servants of the state and the victims tell their specific stories.

If one has witnessed the telling of those stories, as I did at one hearing in South Africa, or watched it in the media, we will resist abstractions and theories from all quarters. If we have heard mothers and fathers weep because they do not know the whereabouts of their "disappeared" sons' bones and cannot bury them properly, we will resist any argument from any political point of view that might try to justify the desecration of a human body.

In stating principles, we should be mindful of particular persons and the specific particles of their existence: the quality of the air they breathe; the purity of the water they drink; the sanitation of the places where they cleanse themselves – "ablutions"; the depth of the drop-holes into which they empty themselves, as so many black South Africans must do in the "locations" and on the farms, which, though they may extend for five or ten thousand hectares, may not provide a flush toilet for the laborers who have worked the land for generations; who, though they may no longer be called "kaffirs" with impunity, still must squat in darkness. We must face these facts if we are to have any credentials as moral observers.

No individual, group, or agency of the state should be able to impinge or intrude upon this boundary without making a legal case against the person who is threatened in this way; and the threatened person should be able to exhaust all legal means, including all recognized standards of international law, to protect himself against incursions into his private world. The real world and the world of realpolitik present many challenges to this principle (including some examples that would be difficult to dismiss), but, on balance, it seems to be the case that more rather than fewer safeguards need to be put between the individual and forces larger than himself.

In South Africa during the apartheid era, the most obvious example of the transgression of this principle was that people were told where and with whom they might live. The state used its power to remove people from their natal ground, told them with whom they might associate and with whom they might work, separated families, dictated vacation periods, imposed laws of travel and transit, and legislated "pass laws." Not until 1994 were Indians allowed to spend more than twenty-four hours in the Free State if they were traveling, say, from Durban to Cape Town.

When I arrived in Johannesburg, the former United States Information Service, which administrated the Fulbright program, was kind enough to arrange for a driver, Amos, to take me to Bloemfontein in a spacious station wagon larger than many South African "shanties." Amos, who was originally from what is now called KwaZulu-Natal, would not stop for a bite to eat during the five-hour drive, no matter how often I suggested that we do so because I was hungry. He kept waving me off, pointing to the endless fields of mealies, saying, "So much land for so few people; I didn't know that there was so much open land."

I realized after I had been in South Africa for a few months that Amos had probably never been in the Free State, and although he had every right to be there for as long as he wished, he wasn't at ease about it. He was wary, perhaps frightened, about getting off the main road, just as white farmers in the Free State have become afraid of farm violence. He took me to my destination, the Faculty of the Humanities, and turned the van around in order to get back to Johannesburg without incident. I assumed it would be a long and anxious drive for him.

The longer I stayed in South Africa, the more aware I became, through my own experience and the media (print and electronic), of possible offenses to the body and how these offenses define the crisis of transformation that is under way in South Africa today. If the body is given short shrift in a consideration of human and social value, then nothing else is likely to be given much value. The Nazis understood, as Terrence Des Pres makes clear in *The Survivor*, that to degrade the body is to degrade the dignity of the person. Once the person's self-worth and humanness have disappeared, killing him becomes almost irrelevant. Each perverse act makes the next thinkable. Two instances of these offenses can serve to exemplify the others that I observed and the countless thousands that took place during the apartheid era:

> When the wife of an elderly Mpumalanga farmer escaped an attack by two men, she thought the worst was over. Then she found her husband Gieljam Otto (81) in the farm's storeroom, with his hands bound, and suffocated on fertilizer ... he had fertilizer stuffed into his mouth and had a cloth wrapped over his mouth and nose. He also had three small stab wounds on his body. (The *Star*, April 16, 1998)

Was he choked on fertilizer or wounded first? Either of the two acts, each heinous, would have sufficed to bring the old man to the ground, if not to his end. One of the two acts was gratuitous, an "extra," a way of saying, "Nothing about your existence is beyond our reach." Killing the farmer, presumably to rob him, becomes inseparable from obliterating his dignity and taking his life. I doubt if the killers thought much about how or even why they were going to kill the farmer, but that is part of the point: the separateness of the other person, the integrity of his boundaries, is often violated before the ultimate violation.

And there is a terrible irony in this, too, for it was precisely separateness of a certain kind that the white world imposed upon the non-white in South Africa under apartheid. Non-white people were forced to live at the edge of the white world.

Eventually, they became strangers to, and estranged from, one another. Once this happened, dignity and humanity became easy targets and casualties. Unless people are entitled to live within sacred boundaries that define their uniqueness and difference from others, without that difference being redefined as something other than an expression of humanness, then all acts become possible.

No book makes this more clear than the account of the state assassin Eugene de Kock, as told to Jeremy Gordin, in *A Long Night's Damage: Working for the Apartheid State*. In his Afterword, Gordin says: "Even though De Kock had contact with many of his victims, their needs and humanity never stood in his way." Eugene de Kock may present an extreme possibility for inhumanity under the apartheid government, but his actions were not unique, save, perhaps, by repetition and his willingness to tell the truth afterward. And the psychological and moral grounds for his action were prepared for by the underlying assumptions of the racial attitudes and laws that characterized the Nationalist Government. As in Nazi Germany, so in South Africa: The extermination of people may have been performed by small numbers of people, relative to the total population, but it was made possible by a dark pre-history of moral degradation. In saying this, I do not imply that the South African government systematically murdered non-white people or planned to do so. It is to say rather that the mentality that made apartheid possible in the forms that it took is not unrelated to the Aryan consciousness that made Hitler and Hitlerism possible. Needless to say, mentality is one thing and acts of collaboration and extermination another. To say that there are anti-Semitic elements in T. S. Eliot is not to accuse him of being a Nazi.

De Kock describes in his book how he killed and eliminated his victims, in this case a former Vlakplaas informant, Johannes Tempa Mabotha, an "askari," who had allegedly become a double agent for the ANC (African National Congress). It is poignant to note the Afrikaans Christian name and the Afrikaans spelling of "Ma-botha." De Kock says:

We went and stood with him at the bottom of a quarry at the Penge mine. Explosives had already been placed there since it had been decided earlier that Mabotha would be taken to the mine, shot dead there, and his body destroyed by explosives. When Mabotha saw the explosives in the ground, he turned around and looked at me. I looked him in the eye and I shot him twice in the heart with a .38 Special revolver. He died immediately. Vermeulen and Snyman took off his clothes, put his body on the explosives and then either Vermeulen or Snyman detonated the explosives. (The Sunday *Independent*, April 5, 1998)

There is no remorse in De Kock's narrative as there may have been no rage in his act of assassination. Mabotha did not exist for him as a person with a heart that beat to his specific rhythms. He was part of a system that had to be eliminated by another system. It is morbidly fitting that the murder and detonation (for that is what it was) of Mabotha should have taken place in a mine, site and symbol of the locus of power in the former South Africa. Cecil Rhodes's "Big Hole" became in time a defining instance of the exploitation of black labor in South Africa as the mines, in general, were key reasons for removing black South Africans from their native regions to work-site "locations." Eventually, the "Big Hole" stood for the moral darkness that gives the lie to certain church pieties.

We need to respect the struggle for existence and subsistence. There is a tendency in South Africa, as elsewhere, to think that people who *have* less than others *are* less than others, that those who earn less than others are less valuable. Needless to say, this works to the advantage of the "haves" since it makes it easier for them to impose further hardships upon the have-nots without guilt.

My experience in South Africa led me to draw the opposite conclusion. I saw specific instances of people, mainly black, struggling to preserve a sense of self- and family-worth within terribly straitened circumstances; and I might add that some of these same people helped me preserve my own sense of self-worth. At a time when I was struggling with large medical bills during a crisis that occurred during my Fulbright year, the "matrons" who attended to my "gaste woonstel" (guest apartment) would remove my 4 x 4 coffee filter bags and set them aside to dry so they could be used again. This small gesture, which I didn't understand at first (why hadn't they thrown them away?) became a moral index for me; and when I returned to Buffalo on half-pay for four months and had to economize as I hadn't previously, I would think fondly of Martha, the head matron, as I weighed the comparative value of buying a tomato against a cucumber. I felt, in some Whitmanesque sense that we were shopping together. She walked beside me in the affluent wilderness of the supermarket.

When I became aware of this act of generous parsimony on my behalf, I started to pay more attention to what black workers would buy in the Brandwag "Kafee" where I did some incidental shopping. One evening, a sturdy man who looked as if he had been working with a pickaxe all day in the veld, helping to prepare the ground for the installation of a bore-hole (the lifeline of the Free State, where wind-pumps make farming possible), bought a minuscule portion of salt, no more than enough for one pinch on one meal – doubtless the meal that he was going to have that night, the only meal that he might be able to afford that day. I looked at him, somewhat quizzically; he held up the little sack and smiled, as if to say, I wanted to think, "It's a good life, I have some salt to put on my mealie-pap."

Dignity is in the details, as well as in the image of man writ large, and I wanted to see the inside of Martha's township house before I left to make sure that she was living above the "dignity line," so to speak. I was apprehensive about making this visit because I had been robbed a few months before in an area where I was vulnerable, but I asked Gary, my usual taxi driver, to take me to her location at midday. He had a two-way radio as well as a Smith and Wesson that he was not afraid to use. He had been a mercenary in the Congo some years before, and his resentment toward the "new South Africa" was sufficiently inflamed that he would protect me, if necessary. His story, his displacement under the post-apartheid government, needs to be told and understood along with the stories of the victimized if reconciliation is to become possible at the lower economic levels.

Gary is a racist and a bigot who blames the ANC for waging a guerrilla war, whereas he was willing to fight in the open like a military man, but he is not trash; his life cannot be set aside. He must be encouraged to tell his story so that, in the telling of it, he may stumble on a disturbing truth, as once he wept telling me something on a ride to Noordstad, or be met with an unexpected response that will lead to new understanding.

Martha met me at the gate of her small compound, where she proudly showed me some newly planted rose bushes. Now that water had been brought to the township, she could spare some for plants. She hopes that one day she may even have a jacaranda tree growing in her yard, invasive as they may be. These trees, which shed their violet and lavender petals like confetti at a Fitzgerald party, would be an extension of her dignity, for they have been associated in South Africa with the lanes and small-holdings of the well-to-do. She has spent part of her life watering the plants of the rich, and she would like to see some growth in her own tiny realm. It is natural for her, as for the Medici or the Nabobs of Hyderabad, to show off her "wealth." She is a good Christian, but she doesn't think that the meek will inherit the earth, as she told me wryly one day; rather she thinks that the poor should inherit as much of the earth as anyone else, since everyone is now equal in the new South Africa.

She showed me, again with pride, where she plans to build another room, for which she has amassed the bricks and corrugated iron, if she can continue to work and put aside some money. She is overweight, as are many Sotho women, and has a slight heart condition. Her veins and arteries do not circulate her blood properly, so her ankles are swollen, and she is somewhat hobbled as she walks. I am not convinced that she will have that extra room, but she now possesses something under the new government: title to her land, ownership of her house, basic utilities, some space, and, she adds, "Windows, I almost forgot. Before, we choked sometimes on paraffin fumes in the winter." Each of her two children has a separate room, and she is pleased that she will be able to bequeath this place, from which they cannot be removed, to them. Now essentially black commanders lead the South African Police Service and Defense Force, so she feels relatively safe. She may be robbed, she might even be killed during a robbery, but she couldn't be taken away if her husband were to visit illegally, as in the past. She says, "My husband died in a mine, but now he could come."

She served me some rooibos tea in her modest sitting room with a proper cup and saucer. Although there is a new South Africa aborning, it will take a long time for Martha to get used to the fact that two people, one white, one black, can have afternoon tea in South Africa without it making a statement, without her feeling the necessity of trotting out her best china, without my feeling the necessity of having Gary, armed, waiting for me down the road. After centuries of having less and being less, of being less and having less, in the eyes of others, if not her own (one often leads to the other), black South Africans have a long walk to dignity, but they are standing on their own two feet now.

My year in South Africa changed me. I no longer could see the quest for dignity as a journey that applies only to the obviously oppressed and downtrodden, the broken and defeated. Like Hemingway, but without his claims to courage, I had come to see that we're all broken in some way. If we accept that truth, we become less lonely and less vulnerable. Hemingway saw the truth, but could not, I believe, accept it.

In the end, he put himself out of pain instead of living with it and finding a way to make a triumph out of defeat – which, ironically, was his great theme. Life and art are related, but they are not the same.

"Color" (an elusive word), in an ideal world, should be a sign neither of pride nor of shame. It should make one neither visible nor invisible in negative or positive terms. One of the constituents of Nelson Mandela's greatness is that he posited a "non-racial society" as a building block of South Africa's future. A person should neither disappear in the field because his skin is brown nor become an emperor just because he is black. I know that I am talking only about an ideal world here, but it's important to keep it in mind as an image. And it should push us to study the role of color in history more assiduously. It is, it seems to me, a little-understood subject that sometimes takes forms at once grotesque and comic.

In May of 1998, a farm worker, Thomas Lebepe, was beaten up by a white farmer who objected to the fact that Lebepe was driving a cart pulled by a pair of donkeys, one white and the other black, with a sign reading: "The new South Africa." According to Lebepe, the farmer shouted, "Hey, this is not kaffir land!" (Sunday *Times*, May 3, 1998). At one level, the incident, because of the disparity between the pairing of the donkeys as a symbol and as a fact, made for humor, and the newspaper headline read, "Two donkeys and an ass," while the caption quipped, "Two animals whose coloring made a white farmer see red." At another level, it is deadly serious. The farm worker was beaten, and he might have been killed.

Color wars, at the level of the individual and the group, have been a common feature of human history. Can they be overcome? I don't know, but I think a first step toward dignity in this area must be to create so much daily interaction between races, if we are forced to use this word (again, an elusive term, given our variety at every level), that we both see and do not see that someone is, say, black, which is to say non-white, so that we can simultaneously register a sense of that specific history and dismiss the notion of that history as wholly determining an individual's identity. We need to find ways to acknowledge the cultural constructions of the past, including color as part of a person's lived experience, without letting those constructions become or stand for the individual.

As an American with a hyphenated identity, Jewish-American, who participates on both sides of the equation without being the sum of its parts and who is not quite like any other American, Jewish or gentile, I believe it is possible to have an identity that is at once historical and existential, unique and communal.

In looking at and listening to someone – not bad for openers in the forum of life – we need to go beyond false distinctions of inner and outer, self and ideology, color and personality; we need to pay attention to the specifics of selfhood. As I told the students at Grey College in Bloemfontein, not long before I left what came to be a "beloved country," and as I had told, in other ways, the students at Christian Brothers' College: we need to enable people to tell the world, at least some corner of it, who they are in such a way that their discrete characters become recognizable; in such a way that knowledge of them becomes possible; in such a way that the inviolate space of self-definition and articulation of consciousness earns respect; in such a way that the State (and all its instruments of law and power) would think twice and three times before it dared infringe upon the sacred rights of self-expression in all its possibilities: speech, writing, gesture, education, access to information and knowledge, as well as economics (being able to purchase the tools and objects of learning).

In effect there needs to be a shift from generic markers of identity to the specifics of personal existence. When Biff says in *Death of a Salesman*, "I'm just what I am, that's all," he is speaking in his own voice; it is a lesson in dignity and democracy. He follows Emerson, Thoreau, and Robert Frost. In saying this, I am not opposing the individual to the community. That is a destructive division. Voices become individual in relation to other voices, a dialogue, and the chorus. We speak a common language, but we speak it uncommonly. "Ubuntu," shared humanity, and self-realization are not incompatible.

And we need to speak directly to others. I lived for ten months in a guest apartment in a women's hostel, Welwitschia, without speaking to the students until the last week. The hostel had become "non-white" through a principle of "voluntary association" – an unhappy index of the difficulty of nation-building in South Africa today. I wanted over the course of the academic year to speak to the students as they walked past the waving plumes of the pampas grass on the way to their side of the hostel, but decorum and self-consciousness stopped me. I was male; I was white. I didn't know what they would make of an overture, but I couldn't imagine leaving their country without speaking to them, just as I couldn't imagine leaving without visiting a few townships, where, after all, the majority of people live. And so I asked the warden to arrange a meeting for me. I wrote a fable, from which I read an excerpt to them: "When the professor arrived in the far-away place, he was pleased to discover that his 'gaste woonstel' was not a cave or a dark hut. He did not meet the young women who were, he was told, preparing to build a new country, but he often heard them at night, singing, playing music, and talking, when he sat out on his terrace when the moon was luminous. He wondered what they were saying. He wanted to tell them that he had come to help them build a new land so everyone could have fresh water and live safely in their own homes...."

They smiled in all the right places, and I knew I had been foolish to be so stand-offish and they had been wrong to think that I would want to stand or sit alone on my terrace. They invited me to a "braai" (cook-out). Some turned out to be interested in writing, and in learning how to publish their work – a universal impulse, I've discovered, for young writers. I told them I had some reference books that might be of use to them.

I shared some of my groaners with them: "Where there's a quill, there's a way," which, in the light of the feathered pampas plumes outside the hostel, made poetic sense, but we all knew that it was too late for us to get much accomplished. Still, it was a start and a lesson, a fable. When I was about to return to America, one of the students called on behalf of the others to thank me for my visit; but, in truth, we had little to say. We hadn't talked enough.

A good deal about the world and South Africa would have to change to enable people to tell who they are in a meaningful way. We would need to change the material and spiritual world, to build classrooms of the future and to re-imagine interior space. It is all too easy for us to negate the being of others. One day I asked the head matron at the university where a certain hard-working matron, who had worked at the university for many years, lived. She looked blankly at me. She had no idea and was surprised, it seemed to me, that I had asked. What difference could it possibly make? She had no interest in the person to whom she gave orders. All she, whoever she was, needed to do was her job. She was her job, so to speak.

So far I have tried to describe the conditions and circumstances that make dignity possible as a matter of our responsibility to others, to say what we, as individuals and a society, need to do to become, in the words of the Anglican liturgy, a "man for Others." I say this with recognition of the horrors of modern history from the Gulag and Robben Island to the killing fields of Cambodia, the villages of Kosovo, and the marsh people of Iraq. I have no illusion that South Africa or the world will be much different in a hundred years from what it is today with respect to man's moral life; but we must act as if it can be.

And no matter what we, the privileged, do, we must, at the end of the day, insist that others, the refused, take their lives into their own hands and dramatize continuously what it means to be human. No image captures this imperative more intimately for me than a prize-winning photograph by Naashon Zalk, exhibited at the Poverty Hearings Photographic Exhibition (1998) sponsored by the South African National NGO Coalition, the Human Rights Commission, and the Commission on Gender Equality. This photograph shows a man reading a book in his "home," an old storm-water drain near Dobsonville in Soweto. His back is somewhat bent, his head grazes the top of the drainpipe, but his fingers touch the page lovingly as he reads by the light at the end of the tunnel. We need to be reminded, through observation, art, media, and the Internet, of all the specific ways in which people struggle to preserve their dignity against great odds. If we observe the hard journey toward dignity that many people make on a daily basis, we may find that our own journey toward dignity is enhanced. To some extent, we give what we are asked to give. Dignity toward others, dignity for ourselves – they are intertwined.

I am reminded, in saying this, of a thrilling moment in the Free State when a friend and I drove one Sunday to a dam outside Bloemfontein. For a country that seems largely parched in many areas, there are surprising depths of waters and catchments; but this is not the metaphor I'm reaching for now. The landscape was typically bare and spare in this fairly arid veld, which requires a Rembrandt to delineate the variety of straw colors. My friend, who has a practiced eye for the subtleties of this landscape, pointed out a row of bishop birds, specks of crimson, sitting on a wire fence against the backdrop of wind-pump, kraal, gum trees, and koppies – the archetypal landscape of the Free State.

As we passed the section of the fence where the birds were perched at intervals of four to six inches, hundreds of them, they all suddenly left their positions in one instant and flew up together to make a large crimson ball that rotated and glistened in the sunlight, a burst of unified radiance that dazzled me. It occurred to me some months later that the flight of these birds was a natural image for the "rainbow nation" that Nelson Mandela dreams of, where individuals, specks in themselves, come together, improbably, to form one brilliant palette that is transcendentally uplifting.

It may seem absurd to say this now in the face of the crime and violence in post-apartheid South Africa; but I believe, nonetheless, that the elements are there to form one nation, one flight of birds. It will take time. I thought of this on my sixty-second birthday as I floated in a mineral pool under the canopy of several majestic blue-gum trees and thought of my relative youth compared to Florisbad man, whose bones and artifacts, embedded in the earth just over the rill from where I swirled, were being studied and curated by a friend at the National Museum in Bloemfontein. She came to the side of the pool, holding a scimitar-shaped tooth. "You're really quite young," she said, smiling.

"And so is the 'new South Africa,'" I returned.

Re-vision

The curtain rises and falls in *Death of a Salesman* to the sound of a flute. The flute serves in the play to sound a note at once plaintive and promising, a reminder of the time when Willy's father sold his hand-made flutes in the "Western states" and an intimation of decline and death. I heard this double melody in my mind's ear at dawn on some days when I sat on my small terrace and thought, in the days before my departure, about the future of South Africa. Before I left Bloemfontein, I went to the top of Naval Hill and looked out at the city and the smallholdings beyond and the koppies in the distance and the shadows of the Maluti Mountains of Lesotho beyond them. I tried to look into the future of the country.

South Africa never can be in the next generation or two the country that it might have been if the National Party had not been elected in 1948 with its apartheid policies, to say nothing of earlier colonial and racist policies, going back to the founding of a shipping station in 1652 by the Dutch East India

Company. Much the same can be said, of course, about America, Mexico, or Brazil – wherever European countries explored and conquered in the sixteenth and seventeenth centuries and imposed inhuman and divisive social, economic, and racial hierarchies.

If the possibilities of brave new worlds were lost, other kinds of histories now become possible, histories that include knowledge about the cost of inhumanity in the long run. If innocent harmony is lost forever, it may be replaced by compassion and understanding in the centuries to come. Something like this happens in American literature where the outcasts often become the visionaries and instruments of moral transformation. I think of Richard Wright, Ralph Ellison, and James Baldwin. Out of the dream of unreason comes reason. Speaking for a people once bartered, battered, and lynched, these writers now hold a central place in the American literary academy, and new generations of students are learning more about the possibilities for humanness than was possible in my generation, the "tranquilized Fifties," to quote the poet Robert Lowell.

All may not be lost if we take the long view: enough is left to build on in new ways. The great herds of antelope that were shot out in the veld in the nineteenth century are gone, but the springbok is the national symbol of South Africa, and these nimble and alert creatures still pronk through the tall grass – their arching leaps a reminder of disaster and promise. On the same day that I went to the top of Naval Hill, I spotted a springbok in the tall grass, and he did not bound away. The creature seemed to know that it was the soul of South Africa and that I longed for a final connection before I left.

I was reminded in that instant of one of my first impressions of South Africa when I observed some men lingering in front of a video store in the Rosebank Mall who were watching a herd of springbok running in circular patterns through the veld. These men seemed out of place in the city. The real South Africa lay elsewhere for them. Needless to say, the country can't go back to its origins. It must invent a future that includes meaningful aspects of the past. This will not be an easy process. It will require anguish and courage to face the pain that one has suffered and inflicted, to feel it without turning inward or striking out. It may be too late.

South Africa is at once a hopeful and a desperate country, but it's too early to cry for the future fate of the country, though not to early to mourn the death of millions of AIDS victims. It may turn out that this disease, not the moral pathology of apartheid, prevents South Africa from becoming a healthy and productive democratic country, but, like Turkey and India, it holds the greatest promise for the reconciliation of nations which are torn apart by racial, religious, and ethnic differences.

During my year in South Africa, my daughter became deathly ill (but, happily, survived to have now three healthy sons); I was robbed and for several hours had no visible proof of identity or material assets; my then four-year-old grandson went missing for an hour during his mother's illness and brought us to the edge of panic and ultimate loss; he also, innocently, threw a rock through the window of my guest apartment and made it clear how easily one's home and property could be destroyed; I temporarily lost two gold crowns and for a half-day felt as if my mouth were an archeological site; I was threatened with a legal case when a landlord thought that I might be a vehicle to alleviate his family's near poverty, and for a brief period I wasn't sure I could leave South Africa as planned and felt imprisoned; and my father died. At a certain point, I was waiting for the locusts to come.

I have lived a privileged life. Being able to live, teach, and write in South Africa was one of those privileges. But it became clear through the threats to my existence at various levels that I was a man among men who could be brought low very quickly. As Freud describes the veneer of civilization that conceals our potential for irrational and aggressive behavior, so one might say that the sense of middle class security is only an illusion as guaranteed circumstance of social life. Think of the Argentineans and Chileans who were "disappeared," of those people who thought that 9/11 would be just another day of work in the World Trade center, of all those non-combatants who have been casualties in the fog of war.

One doesn't have to be a moral philosopher to see that one's own existence is based on a set of assumptions that can be reversed in a second. It would not take much for us all to feel as powerless as Amos and Martha if history or an onrushing truck or an incoming Katyusha missile were to swerve towards us, to say nothing of everyday personal and professional disappointments that can make us feel very quickly that we are worth little to ourselves or others. We are all fellow travelers on the road to dignity.

CHAPTER ELEVEN

HOME AND AWAY:
CONFESSIONS OF AN AMERICAN TRAVELER BETWEEN NEW YORK CITY AND FINLAND

I began to write about my abbreviated trip to Finland in October of 2000 on December 7 of that year, a memorable date, the anniversary of Pearl Harbor (1941), the beginning of World War II against the Axis Powers (Japan and Germany). Freud says somewhere that nothing is trivial in mental life, so perhaps there was some significance to the fact that I began to reflect on my somewhat anguished trip to Finland on a date that is associated with conflict and anxiety for any sentient American of my generation.

I was born on November 5, 1936, and I recall first seeing my mother cry on December 7, 1941, as we listened to the radio and heard President Roosevelt deliver his famous "day of infamy" speech. This was an emotionally charged period for me. No theory of human development has yet discovered a way to make proper use of history, though some have tried; but we know that it's important. I have been trying for half a century to discover the intersection of private and public experience, the interface of consciousness and history.

The great surprise for me is not that I curtailed my trip to Finland and the Baltic region, but that I stayed in other places for much longer periods of time as part of academic commitments and obligations. For reasons that remain largely obscure to me, despite many years of self-analysis, I felt quite alone as a child. Still, some things are clear. My family was not very cohesive, and so I didn't feel that I belonged to a solid entity. Indeed, neither my mother nor father ever used the word "family."

My father had worked himself out of the poverty of the Lower East Side Jewish world of Manhattan and remained preoccupied with work all his life, forty-seven years of it (1923-1970). Fear of poverty and little else entered his consciousness. Gambling, womanizing, and hanging out with his cronies were his main diversions. He didn't look to his home for primary satisfactions. He fulfilled his primary obligations as a provider, but probably felt that he was being held back from some vague destiny.

When frustrated, he would talk of leaving. He would say, in moments of anger, "I'm going to California." Oddly and sadly, he never did go to California. In fact, he went only to Miami Beach one week a year. He often stayed out late, but he never left. He dreamed of flight, but stayed. Some primitive instinct, a product of immigrant anxiety, told him to stay put once you had established an economic basis for survival.

My mother was a provincial girl. She grew up in near poverty in a Pennsylvania railroad town, where her father worked for the Pennsylvania Railroad, and came to New York City as a teenager with her family when her father lost his job. She met my father on the subway (A-Train) and decided to get married in order to leave the confines of an unhappy home. Her mother was ungiving and stingy, she says. My father was a "giver," at least in financial terms. That was obvious to her.

She knew that she had made an unhappy marital choice after six months, but she didn't want to return home. Within eight years, she had two sons. She devoted herself to these two boys. They gave her the love she needed. She turned to movies and movie magazines for romance. My mother knew more about Ronald Coleman's life than he probably knew himself.

She dreamed, too, of going to California, but stayed. Trapped, but secure, she moved in reverie. This is perhaps one coordinate of human existence and half my psyche as well.

I should qualify this. She did leave once or twice for a day or so, but she always returned to her sons. I never really believed that she would leave, but the fantasy of her leaving affected me deeply. Often, after school, I would check the closet to see if her fur coats, prized in those days, were still there. I thought, for some reason, that she would not leave without her mink coat, symbol of middle-class success in the postwar era. I was probably right.

My mother's occasional flight from domestic tensions (fueled by my father's infidelities) may well have contributed to my becoming a writer-traveler. I recall a specific day when this transformation may have taken place. I was about thirteen years old, just after my Bar Mitzvah. My parents had argued in the evening. When I returned from school the next day, my mother was not there. A note said that she would be away for a while but would return soon. But how "soon"?

It was a rainy spring afternoon, and I walked to the schoolyard, knowing that my mother would return, but convinced in that moment that I wouldn't see her again. It seemed to me that I was alone in the schoolyard. The world outside of the fence looked like another world, a strange world, but a world with people in it. The schoolyard was a second home to me, but now it felt alien. I felt that I would be safe only if I went further afield to Broadway and 181st Street where people swirled around, shopping, lining up for the movies at the local movie palace, the Coliseum. Then, I would belong somewhere.

I turned up the collar of my trench coat and felt oddly grown-up, a writer-to-be, someone who would observe the world at a distance and would struggle to overcome that distance and make it a version of home. "Home" was familiar, but full of conflict and the anxiety of abandonment; "away" represented a displacement, but also the promise of community

– unknown, uncertain, but beckoning. If I were lucky, it occurred to me, I might create a community in and through writing. One could draw together and move among versions of people who otherwise would have no knowledge of one another. I had begun to read Thomas Wolfe, before he was discredited by the postwar New Critical atmosphere, and could identify with some of the emotions and thoughts swirling around inside of his huge work.

I walked down Ft. Washington Avenue toward 181st Street, the 42nd Street of our neighborhood in Washington Heights, the northern edge of what has been called Frankfurt on the Hudson, to which many exiles and refugees from Nazi Germany had come. Some old war posters were still pasted on billboards: "Join the Navy and See the World"; "Uncle Sam Wants You!" "The Marines Can Use a Few Good Men." These signs lifted my spirits. I lost myself in the crowd at the movie, watching Humphrey Bogart in *Casablanca*. My father was home early when I returned. Perhaps my mother had called him. He assured me she would be back soon. He pulled out an old map book and asked me where places were in the world, our only game. My mother soon returned, but I never was quite the same.

So: my father threatened to leave, but never left; my mother, never threatening or angry, left a few times out of an unspoken frustration and unhappiness that I only could guess at. Both dreamed of an escape: he, to a world where no one would make demands upon him, where he could satisfy his appetites without complicated acts of sharing; she, to a world of movie magazines – tropical landscapes, moonlight shining on the water, ocean liners with orchestras, tuxedo-clad lovers with bouquets of roses. She would be Anna Karenina or Ninotchka. I should say that the marriage improved in their later Florida years. Eventually, after more than half a century, my mother referred to my father as her "best friend," and my father's greatest drive near his death was to leave my mother in a financially secure position.

My older brother, in the light of this parental situation, was a nervous and restless child. As the first-born, he reacted sensitively to his young mother's uncertainties – married at eighteen, a mother at twenty-one. A bright and imaginative child, a reader as well, he discovered through books – Kipling, Jules Verne, Rider Haggard – that there were places to which one could go to escape domestic tensions. He took the subway to the Bronx Zoo; he went to the University of Wisconsin, first member of our family to cross the Hudson River; he hitch-hiked to Hollywood during college; he ended up, finally, living in Portugal, practicing law in a country he and his wife had grown to love, where he has been for the past thirty years (he, too, got the message, apparently, about staying put).

In the light of these typical, but determining influences, the surprise is that I ever left Buffalo for long periods of time to teach overseas, for I always felt as if I were tempting psychological fate in some way, crossing some emotional or mental border — making a reckless choice, which would leave me stranded — from beyond which I wouldn't be able to return.

But I did go, somehow, to Ankara, Turkey, 1983–84, as a Fulbright scholar at Ankara University; Kuala Lumpur, 1988, as a professor of American literature in my home university's (SUNY/Buffalo) extension program in Malaysia; Hong Kong, 1991–94, as a lecturer in the Department of English at Hong Kong University; Bloemfontein, South Africa, 1998, as a Fulbright professor of American literature in the University of the Free State. Driven by vanity (bourgeois literary academics like me were supposed to be travelers) and impelled to gather material for writing, anchored in Buffalo, New York, a livable place but not New York City or Boston, I forced myself to go out and see the world.

What special factors came into play during my trip to Finland? I'm not sure that there were singular ones. It was more a culmination of a long history, the unfolding of many themes and motifs, a partial eruption of my psyche and the unearthing of a profound need to have a real home. My inability to stay in Finland probably began when I left Buffalo on October 5 and bade farewell to my daughter and, perhaps more importantly, in this instance, my grandson, who had lived with me, on and off, since he was an infant.

I was, in effect, his surrogate father at that time, so my leaving was a double loss for both of us. Having had a brief marriage (two years), my significant experience of family had been raising, as a single parent, my daughter for a decade and then helping her, as a single parent, raise her son, my grandson – who often enough looked like my father, my mother, my brother, myself, even as he always looks like himself. Given this special relation to my daughter and grandson, I was, in leaving them, leaving whatever I had known securely of family experience.

But leave I must, or so it seemed. After all, I was on sabbatical. I had told people I would be traveling. I had woven a little Marco Polo mythology around myself. I promised to bring stories back from away places. In the act of leaving, I already was shaping stories I would tell when I returned. Listening to me, you would have thought that I was Lawrence of Arabia or Somerset Maugham. But I didn't tell people how hard leaving and staying, being home and going away, always had been for members of – can I say it? – my family.

I flew to New York City in order to attend a banquet at the New York Public Library, the great columned building on Fifth Avenue and 42nd Street, which stood in my childhood, as it has doubtless for countless native New Yorkers, as a monument to writing and learning. One of the dreams of my early adolescence, at the point where I thought of myself as a would-be writer, was to have a book of mine housed in this imposing structure, this American Parthenon.

I had realized this dream. Indeed, more than one of my books was in the library's collection; but I had not yet become – might never become – the important American writer that I wished to be. The banquet – to honor participants in a series of lectures surrounding the library's new exhibit, "Utopia: the

Search for the Ideal Society in the Western World" – both affirmed and denied the fact that I had become the person I dreamed of being in my early adolescence when I was imprinted with the imprint of the Modern Library editions that stood for achievement at that time, the 1950s, in America.

In fact, just about everything leading up to my departure for Finland a day later affirmed and denied my hidden "ego ideal" (as the psychologist Karen Homey calls it). I had asked an old friend, a diplomat, to come up from Washington to join me. We met at the Princeton Club where she was staying, near Grand Central Station and the site of the old Biltmore Hotel.

"Ellen" – let me call her that – was gracious, cordial, funny, and unassuming, as always, the last person in the world to imagine that I would be a little socially self-conscious because she was staying at the Princeton Club while I would be staying (sleeping, really) at Habitat (for "urban nomads," as the brochure says) on East 57th Street. I had chosen Habitat because it seemed to be a smart-looking, inexpensive hotel in a good location; but the brochure had promised more than it delivered, and my small room with bathroom in the hallway had more the feel of a YMCA in the provinces than the sort of place I wanted to be staying after the great banquet on the eve of my departure for Finland.

The banquet was quite elegant: red roses matching the crimson tablecloths; chandeliers, suspended from a wood-beamed ceiling, a simulation of a Tudor hall, the kind of dining room that one would expect to find in one of the stately homes of England or a Cambridge college. It seemed to me that I was surrounded by museum-quality furniture.

My friend and escort, Ellen, spoke animatedly all evening at another table with someone who turned out to be one of the most important and influential editors in America, someone who, if he published my work, could help my literary reputation considerably. It seemed ironic that I hadn't sat next to him, but, if I had, I doubtless would have said nothing about my work, wary of embarrassing either of us. I merely introduced myself at the end and told him that he had made an important contribution to American intellectual life. He was pleased, modest, and somewhat amused. "But," he said, "most of the people here don't read the magazine."

He was probably right. He saw them more clearly than I did because he saw them from the inside looking out. I was still an outsider. I wondered, and wonder, if this feeling would change if and when I scale that fence, a version of that one in the schoolyard, and become the person-writer I dreamed of being at age thirteen. I wanted to ask him what it felt like to be on the other side, but the question would make me too vulnerable. So much of life seems to be a matter of unasked questions, of us, of others.

When we left the library, walking down the steps between the lions (Patience and Fortitude) toward Fifth Avenue, the editor, wearing a black tuxedo, stepped into a chauffeur-driven black Mercedes with a woman in a long black dress on his arm. He, the woman, and the car looked like a *New Yorker* ad for vodka. Unfazed by any image of opulence of success, Ellen smiled broadly and waved goodbye to them. My closeness to a certain kind of life both affirmed and denied my life within a second; and then the second passed, but the feeling went down deep and probably stayed there all the way to Finland. Writing and existence were related terms for me.

Lying in bed in my shoe-box-size room in Habitat, looking at a neon-silver sky through a narrow, dusty window, I wondered if I would be able to sleep. This was, I realized, the first time I ever had stayed alone in a hotel in my own hometown, or "lost city," as Fitzgerald calls it, though he had fewer claims than I to belonging to Gotham. I was a true son of Manhattan.

After my parents left New York in 1970 and retired to Florida, I felt as if I had lost my home, even though I had lived out of New York, really, since 1962, when I went to Boston to try out teaching as a possible career. After 1970, I was an exile in Manhattan. I looked at The City, then, as I had looked at the world through the schoolyard fence. It was no longer something I possessed; I now had to reach out for it and hope that I might grasp it again for a moment.

I had this sense of repossession, as it were, when I visited New York over the years with my young daughter, to whom I could show "my city," and with one woman in particular who was eager to share with me the landscape of my lost youth and adolescence. Sad to recall, this first real love, the one who came to me, in the wake of separation and divorce, after eight years of yearning, wrote to say a few months after she had left me for someone else in a university town that "I always would associate New York with you; it always will be your city for me." These were touching words and, of course, I recall them when I go to the city. I look for her and wonder how often, if ever, she has looked for me on the streets we walked together, including the great street I stayed on, 57th Street, on the eve of my departure for Finland.

Tossing and turning in my shoe-box of a room, a proper set for a Beckett play ("Rockaby") or a Kafka fable, I tried to go back through the years to discover the lodestone of loss, a moment of primary displacement that must underlie my enduring sense of loss. But I could do no better than think of a number of significant moments in childhood. The essence of personality does not yield its mysteries like an archeological find, as Freud analogized; and, even if there are shards and fragments, their outlines blur in the sea of early consciousness. It made more sense to build a future than to try to recover a lost past, so I thought of what awaited me in Finland.

It was perhaps unfortunate that my plane didn't leave until mid-afternoon. That gave me the morning to kill, to face the reality of my aloneness in the city. I called an old high-school friend, a deal-maker, who puts together international joint ventures. He cordially invited me to his Fifth Avenue co-op, which overlooks the Pulitzer Fountain and the Plaza where we had held our Senior Prom. This was the first time, I think, that I had looked out at Fifth Avenue from the inside. I always had been on the street; looking up, trying to imagine what it would mean or would have meant to see life in America from the privileged point of view.

I didn't wholly approve of my old friend's life. The bottom of his mind is like the floor of the New York Stock Exchange after a day of busy trading. But he belonged in the city in a way that I didn't, and he knew how much he was worth on a daily basis. He only has to check the value of his company's stock on the NYSE to know if he is worth more or less than yesterday. I would not change places with my friend, but he is more certain of his place in the world than I am. His materialism affirms contrastively the value of my teaching and writing; but the value of his real estate challenges the fragile status of my literary identity.

Our days would be very different. He would walk down to his office at 30 Rockefeller Plaza and see how he best could move some money around the world so that it would come back and make him richer than when it left. I would fly out into the world, looking to add to my sense of self-worth and well-being by finding a community that would make me feel whole, unlike the problematic world of my childhood, the literary academy, or the literary marketplace. I had felt some of this wholeness during my Fulbright year in Turkey, where being "welcomed" is a key fact of social life; and I had experienced it in India, as well.

Looking back, I can see that I probably should not have boarded the Finnair flight for Helsinki with a connection to Oulu. It was a risky choice, but I had come too far, bade too many farewells, to turn back, and, given my ability in the past to come out on the other side of anxiety, I had no reason not to have some belief in myself. And I had lived too long with the apprehension that I might not be able to go anywhere again if ever I succumbed to something like panic for me not to press on.

The Helsinki Airport, wonderfully up-to-date and efficient, high tech to the max, seemed oddly silent and empty when I arrived in the morning. As I made my way through the tube connecting the international and domestic terminals, it was as if I were entering a land of silence. Still, I was carried forward by the hope of finding a new and warm community waiting for me in the small city of my academic destination – Oulu; and I had exchanged some friendly letters with a senior professor in the Department of English, an expert in children's literature, myth, and the origins of consciousness. She would be waiting for me. I knew also that she was recently divorced; and I had sensed in our exchange of letters over the period of almost a year that, like many Scandinavians, few of the varieties of love, sex, and romance were alien to her. Living, as I did, in the often frigid zone of Buffalo, it was not hard for me to imagine that she, living near the more frigid zone of Lapland, might well crave the closeness of a warm body and sympathetic heart.

I arrived at the Oulu airport on a mid-Saturday afternoon in mid-October in the midst of a classic dreary fall day, fraught with intimations of winter: Grey sky, cobalt blue at the western edge, a chill rain; but the air was wonderfully fresh as I walked across the tarmac. It had a touch of Maine and Oregon in it. "Nanna," holding up a modest sign, was waiting me for me, warmly bundled in a typical Suomi outfit, Marimekko, I supposed. I am the sort of American for whom all Finnish music is composed by Sibelius and all clothes designed by Marimekko. I took comfort in her looking snug, but I felt a coldness in my soul, as if the legendary Lapp winter were about to descend upon me. We were only a few hours south of the Arctic Circle.

Sensing some discomfort on my part, Nanna let me know that she had arranged for me to stay in a private apartment, away from students, with a view of a small lake, so I would be able to get some writing done in my free time. "It even has its own sauna," she added. She would loan me a laptop, as well, and show me how to use it. She suggested that I first get settled and then that we take a short drive to a park where I could get some immediate sense of the unique quality of the Finnish air. That seemed a good idea to me. I was eager to spend some time with her, sensing that I would be anxious alone.

The apartment was perfectly adequate, but it felt alien, of course, but then I had learned from decades of travel that I should not judge how I feel about a place until I have spent at least one night there. One's impression in the morning, particularly if the sun is shining, is often quite different from the apparent strangeness of a first evening. I have learned for the same reason that it's better for me to arrive in a new city at dawn. Indeed, I often had thought of writing a little book, *Cities at Dawn.*

I unpacked quickly, a little nervously, knowing that I would be more comfortable returning to a somewhat settled place with the first imprint of a "lived-in" atmosphere. Nanna was patient and intuitive. "I know what it feels like to be in a new place," she said, "I myself have recently moved into a new apartment by myself. If it weren't for my little cottage, I'd be at a great loss. I'll take you there tomorrow, if you wish; you can relax before your first program Monday morning." Her directness was welcome and comforting. I knew that I couldn't be in the hands of a better person.

We drove in her new BMW – Finnish academics seemed to me to live pretty well – past small Lego-looking subdivisions, habitable geometries, toward a pleasant wooded area, where we then walked over aromatic planks, newly cut, that connected a series of fast-rushing streams over outcroppings of rock. I thought of Frost's "West-Running Brook" and some lines in it: "It is this backward motion toward the source, / Against the stream, that most we see ourselves in, / The tribute of the current to the source. / It is this in nature we are from. / It is most us." I quoted these lines to Nanna. She told me how delighted she had been as a high-school student to learn that there was an American nature poet named Frost. It was her first sense, she said, that Americans did something other than make Coca Cola and send people to the moon. "And go to war," I added.

I felt, walking across the planks, that I was, to some extent, walking the plank. The planks represented the scaffolding of my selfhood – the structure I had built to keep me intact in the world – and the roiling waters below were the hidden and unconscious currents that pushed against the pilings of the ego, Coleridge's "I AM."

We exchanged pleasantries as we walked. Nanna told me about my academic program in the week to come and asked me about my plans after I left Oulu. How many days would I spend in Helsinki? Did I want to see the Baltic countries? Did I plan to go to St. Petersburg? She knew, she said, that I had a Russian-Lithuanian background and would want to see that part of the world. These had been my plans, but I knew that I would not act on them. I now was, literally, taking one step at a time. She must have sensed the precariousness of my position.

"I'm alone, too," she said, "after so many years of marriage. My work has taken me too far afield. He's a good man, but a banker. We don't speak the same language anymore. I'm somewhat anxious, but I feel free, too. I'm lucky. I belong here, but I have a new life in front of me and, of course, I have my little cottage. I've written to you about that. It means a great deal to me. It's my 'place apart,' as Frost calls it, I believe. It's where I keep my self. You'll see."

Her "little" cottage, I assumed, would be like the "little" soups that one of my gourmet friends in Buffalo makes, perfect in all ways, but unassuming. I was eager to see it. In fact, I was tempted to ask her to take me there immediately, but several kinds of decorum and restraint prevailed. For all my commitment to being honest and self-revealing to others, I knew as well as anyone else the necessity "to prepare a face to meet the faces that you meet" (T. S. Eliot, "The Love Song of J. Alfred Prufrock").

"You must be hungry and tired," she said, "we'll go to a lively restaurant in town where there's music, and then I'll take you to your place. You may want to do some writing."

We went to a cabaret near the center of town, "rotuaari," where Nanna told me it was appropriate for single women to find dance partners. It was "tango night," she added. This lifted my spirits. I had arrived in Istanbul six months before on tango night at the Armada Hotel on the Sea of Marmora and seen exquisite Turkish women dance with elegant gentlemen. We were among the first to arrive. In fact, not many came after us; and it was clear that tango night at the Metropole would not be like tango night at the Armada on the terrace roof in view of the Blue Mosque.

I lost my appetite, which didn't come back while I was in Finland, but I ate a few morsels of a reindeer dish (what else!), so as not to offend Nanna. And then I asked her to dance, since I knew she would not have brought me to this place unless she had wanted to "trip the light fantastic," as we used to say in high school. As my muscles recalled the lost rhythms of the foxtrot and rumba, I felt as if I were, again, a sexually deprived adolescent in one of the Broadway dance halls of the 1950s. Although I was no Fred Astaire, Nanna seemed pleased.

When she left me off a few hours later at my guest room at my apartment, she had no reason to think that my stay in Oulu would be troubled in any way. She shook my hand, and told me she would "fetch" me mid-morning. I felt that I was on the edge of an anxiety attack when she left, something I had experienced often in my life, but I had techniques for managing these sudden feelings of frightening aloneness and lack of self-worth (they were related), which usually took the form of something like a momentary threat to my identity.

I wanted most when she left to call my daughter and grandson in Buffalo, but I discovered, to my dismay, that there was no telephone in the apartment. Here I was in the land of Nokia, the most "cellular" country in the world, and I couldn't, at least this night, make a call. I took a swig of brandy and turned on the sauna, hoping that the dark moment would pass. There was TV, and that was a comfort. Much to my relief, Deutsche Welle had programs in English, and I was able, partially, to feel part of the world again.

I passed through the moment of crisis, but I couldn't sleep easily, another symptom that didn't pass until I left Finland,

and I found myself working on a chart about the structure of my life, something like the one in Sheaffer's *O'Neill: Son and Playwright*. It was in making this chart that I came up with the paradoxes of my parents' lives and its effect on mine that I describe earlier in this essay about leaving and staying, home and away: home always would feel somewhat alien; strange worlds offered the promise of community.

I had some hope that I had found the key to the locked door of my unconscious. I was too much of an old-fashioned Freudian to give up completely the Sherlock Holmesian notion that a rational explanation lies beneath every mystery. I remained, to some extent, a sleuth in relation to my own mental life. And there was no doubt that I had made a discovery, perhaps even an important one for me – a foundational blueprint of my psychological life; but the life of consciousness seems to have no origin or terminus, no definite beginning.

I was able, after a few more swigs, to fall asleep, at least for a few hours. I prayed that I would awake, flooded in sunshine, a new man; but it was not to be. The day broke gray and remained so. The land of the Midnight Sun was heading toward midnight at dawn, it seemed. I put up some coffee and turned on classical music, but I had no impulse to write. That was not a good sign. I tried a few postcards, but didn't get further than addresses (they remain in the archive of my abbreviated trip). Writing requires a measure of hope and self-confidence, and I wasn't feeling much of either on this Finnish morning which felt more like mourning, as did the small lake, a few hundred yards beyond some berry fields, that I could see over the bicycle path that passed by the apartment house in which I was lodged, or imprisoned, as it felt on this morning. One small fishing boat lay wedged between some rocks. It reminded me of a painting I saw a few days later in Oulu's art museum – Torsten Wasastjerna's "Strand med bat" (1887), a Manet-like study of isolation and desolation.

Embarrassing, as it is to admit, I felt like that boat. I hoped my mood would change when Nanna came to pick me up at midday, but I was on edge when she arrived. She sensed my mood, and as we drove to her cottage, with a baroque CD playing (academic taste crosses borders), she put her hand on top of mine, lightly. "It will be OK, we have a lot in common, we'll talk, and you'll feel better. Give it a chance." *Give it a chance.* It was a phrase that resonated all the time that I was anxious in Finland.

Nanna's cottage was the perfect realization of all the Bergman films I ever had seen, with touches of Hollywood-Adirondack comfort: hewn beams, oil-lamps, hand-woven rugs and blankets, iron kettles; and all the ingredients for making a fire were on hand, sweet-smelling tinder in a copper bucket, long matches. Cliche or archetype? It was hard to tell.

I asked her if I could make the fire, and she smiled in assent. Soon we were lying next to one another on the rug, our heads propped on reindeer-fur bolsters. We could see the small, private lake through the floor-to-ceiling windows. The sky was light blue, edged with violet. A few cottage lights were on across the lake. I thought of a childhood camp in Kent, Connecticut, foothills of the Berkshires, when I first had seen this transforming scene and heard music over the water.

"It's a lovely and lonely place to be," I said.

"Just like the fairy tales. I've spent twenty years studying them. Those stories and this scene are part of my soul, my children. Yours, too, I think. Usually I don't need anything else." She leaned against me, drawing my head to her breasts, waiting for a response. Vulnerable in my loneliness, I wanted to lose myself in her, but I knew that, after, I might feel a greater sense of distance, separation. I had failed at intimacy so many times and intimacy had failed me often enough.

An exile from the great maternal bond, it was easier and less threatening for me to connect myself to the world through writing than it was to reach out for love. Sex was easier, but not here. Nanna was my host, and I had a week of lectures ahead of me. I had to keep my balance. I had to step back from the brink. I wasn't in Kuala Lumpur and Hong Kong, where I could find release with a masseuse in the hands of a practiced concubine for hire.

"You're the perfect host," I said. "Emerson would have loved you."

"Emerson?"

"The beginning of *Nature:* 'Embosomed for a season in nature, whose floods of life stream around and through us.'" It was perhaps a foolish thing to say, but perhaps better than acting in a foolish way.

"Yes, I know that passage. I've quoted it in my work, believe it or not. Nature doesn't ask anything from us; it never disappoints us. I understand. Let's have a swim and sauna. The world will seem different after."

"Swim?"

"Well, go in."

I had opened my mouth about nature. Now I was trapped. Besides, I couldn't let her down about this. "Here," she said, getting up, "here's a robe for you. I'll change inside."

We walked Indian file, each holding a hurricane lamp, to the edge of the lake, whose dark surface was barely distinguishable from the bank. Nanna put her robe on a wooded peg on the side of the sauna cabin and slipped into the water without a sound. I felt that I had failed to meet her offer of intimacy and would fail other tests. The least I could do now would be to join her in this freezing baptism that would, somehow join us.

And, if nothing else, there would be comic relief. "Here goes my American manhood," I said and jumped into the water, howling. Somehow we ended up face to face, arms around one another, with an exhilarating and penetrating recognition that we had thrown all academic caution to the winds, or frigid currents, and would be unable ever to lie to one another.

"Look," she said, "I've never seen that before." A small group of reindeer moved along the shore on the far side of the lake, the outlines of their bodies clear against the last vestiges of twilight. "You've seen Finland." I once had seen some deer prancing along a road near where I live, but I knew they were foraging, forced out of a narrowing habitat. This herd was free to roam in pristine forests.

In the sauna, a few minutes later, I told her many things about my life, including much of what I've written here, and she told me a great deal about herself. We realized that we were, for different reasons, more committed to childhood and children in life and legend that we ever could be to one another. We had looked for love in and through our work for too many years. Like many academics and writers, we had found too many compensations by moving in the ether of words to come down to earth now. In any case, it made no sense to try for too much here. Too much was at stake professionally. Still, I hoped that the sudden closeness between us, the naked encounter, would put my anxieties to rest. We walked back toward the warm glow of the cottage. I considered myself blessed, if only for a moment.

As we drove back to my apartment, I realized that the connection between Nanna and me was like my relationship to overseas travel. It came to me as a kind of formula that I now can align with other themes in this investigation: *far, but near; near, but far*. I had traveled far from Buffalo to the remote city of Oulu (as, indeed, Buffalo must seem remote to Oulu) only to discover that a true sense of belonging would elude me again. I had come close to the kind of reunion that I must have imagined as a possibility when I looked through that schoolyard fence at age thirteen, but only close.

It was tempting to think that the problem lay with Oulu. I was in a minor city again – not Helsinki. As I had been in Ankara, not Istanbul; as I had been in Bloemfontein, not Cape Town; as I had been in Buffalo, not New York City. I was in a minor city because I was a minor writer; I was a minor writer because I had spent four decades in a minor city. But this kind of self-punishment was just a smoke screen for deeper layers of disappointment that lay in family history –

layers that I had unearthed, to some extent, in the chart that I had traced out in Oulu.

And it was possible that my feelings had something to do with being the grandson of an immigrant, with the particular history of my family. To make it in America, to assimilate, was to separate oneself from one's origins. In the act of learning to speak standard, academic, and, even literary, American English, my brother and I had put a distance between our grandparents and us and, to a lesser, but significant, extent, our parents. Having mastered the American language, my brother and I were able to cross borders and frontiers in an effort to become successful.

In fulfilling our parents' ambitions for us, we put a distance between ourselves and their lives in New York and, later, in Florida. We had sought an escape from the limited environments of our childhood. But escape creates a longing for home. My mother, a sometimes-exile, always came home; my father, enslaved to labor in New York's garment industry, never left. My brother, like my mother, left and never came back, but dreams of home. I, a civil servant of sorts, stay in one place more or less, and dream of ending my exile from New York City, but I shall doubtless stay. The four of us, always, would be at once out of place wherever we were – home and away.

These paradoxes were somewhat overwhelming to contemplate on the return from our naked encounter, but I hoped that their essential clarity would give me some peace of mind and let me sleep deep and hard so that I would be in full possession of myself as I began a week of lectures. But I awoke in a cold sweat, having dreamed that my grandson had forgotten my name. This reminded me of another dream, decades earlier, in which I had seen my daughter – separated from me by a continent – calling out for me silently. I had awakened not knowing what she wanted or needed. I had written a poem, "Summer's End," about it:

A Barbie doll, waterlogged and naked,
Lips sealed to a hardened stem, still
Drifts through the black water in the Port
Bottle ledged against your empty bed.
You always leave an after-image, dreams:
I touch your hair floating upwards
As you sink, mute, mouthing my name.

My grandson had been the bulwark of my emotional life since I had returned from Hong Kong in 1994. We had slept head to toe in a circle of love on many winter nights when icicles as long as broadswords virtually imprisoned us. In South Africa, in the midst of a crisis in which I had feared detainment, I had been afraid to listen to a tape of his then two-year-old voice, unsure, irrationally, if I ever would see him again.

It was clear, waking up in Oulu, with a surreal sense that I was no longer in his life, that I had come to the brink of a collapse. I had to admit to myself that I had a need greater than any academic or literary or vain social ambition. I knew that I would have to leave Oulu and Finland earlier than I had planned if I wished to avoid a crack-up of some kind. If jet lag came into the equation, it was not possible for me to sort it out from other feelings at three in the morning so far from home.

I told Nanna in the morning, when she came to pick me up, that I had decided to return earlier than planned to America. I said that I was in the midst of some kind of mental crisis. I assured her that I would be able, nonetheless, to fulfill my academic obligations with the loan of her Nokia cell-phone and her support. She listened to what I was saying and did not question me. I gave many lectures during the ensuing week and spoke with many people, every word girded by will and pride. Fortunately, I had written out all the words, so, even in moments when I felt like fleeing, I could focus on a text and tame my impulses; and there were saving moments when the Finnish world grabbed my imagination.

a safe heaven in which to long for, and mourn, one's lost origins. This aspect of Jewish history is a metaphor for all people and the Jew a symbol of all men.

We live our life in stages, as well as one stages one's life, and these stages becomes layers, the self becoming, in time, as much an archeological site as an archival storehouse of memory. In fact, in visiting these sites in the somewhat Holy Land (Beit She'an, Caesarea, Capernaum, Masada, the Old City of Jerusalem, Rosh Pina), the archeological analogy becomes compelling; but it is just another simile for the formation of identity.

I am more interested now in general culture and international relations now than I am in individual psychology; or, it might be more accurate to say that I am interested in what I might call "cultural autobiography." This collection of essays has been at attempt to find the meeting point of these two terms and to show their interdependence.

CHAPTER TWELVE

OF TRAVEL, EDUCATION, AND WRITING

*T*he site and location of one's writing is important. I took notes for this essay on the reedy banks of the Sea of Galilee one summer at the meeting point of many Western and Eastern influences, and what I have to say finally about travel and writing, especially world travel, is connected to my understanding of, and response to, the violent struggles in the Middle East today. The anxiety of taking a bus in Israel and the pleasure of exchanging splashes with an Israeli-Arab child in the sacred Kinneret shape my views about cultural difference and individual differences within culture in general, as does the landscape of the Lower Galilee: bougainvillea, olive groves, eucalyptus, flame trees, oleander, date palms, cypress – to say nothing of the sere hills and the radiant light edging Mount Arbel at dusk: natural equivalents of the political and moral chiaroscuro of that troubled part of the world.

By world travel, I mean mainly living overseas in order to teach and/or teaching overseas in order to live and to write. I have done a certain amount of freelance traveling over the years, beginning with a European "grand tour" in 1956–57, but my most meaningful experiences have been the by-products of affiliations with overseas institutions of higher learning and the many opportunities for travel and lecturing that grew out of these affiliations.

No Marco Polo or Paul Theroux, I nonetheless have, in the words of an old song, "traveled across the gravel." And if there is one thing (or set of things) that I have learned that has profound implications for writing and education, it is, most simply and complexly, obviously and most subtly, that *people are different in relation to their different cultures,* to say nothing of their uniqueness. To face and accept difference in all of its perceived and recreated particularities is the challenge and wonder of travel; to try to give articulate texture to this generalization is the writer's privilege and burden. Travel in the non-Western world confronts you up close and personal with what leading thinkers and intellectuals have been arguing for a few decades: only an awareness of, and respect for, difference can make our world less violent. We must resist all totalizing abstractions: ideologies, theologies, and national myths.

This is easy enough to say, but what a writer needs to store for future writing often comes through hard and uncomfortable experience: driving through a monsoon rain in an open auto-rickshaw to find a hotel with an overhead fan so that you won't wake up at four in the morning and spend the rest of the Orissa night wondering if there might be a cobra in your room; getting a fungal infection in the Malaysian jungle because you wanted to see what a real village ("kampong") looked like; tramping through narrow back-streets in Guangdong Province with an aching lower back because you want to see firsthand just how advanced the PRC is; talking with a stranger, as a stay against loneliness in Chengdu, to whom you cannot say tender things in a common language.

These are just some commonplace examples of what you do to gain knowledge when you're far from home and looking for enlightenment in a far away place. If you wish to expand your anthropological repertoire, with its educational implications, and to escape what Walter Pater calls the "thick wall of personality," a writer-traveler needs to observe and absorb other lives in other contexts. Again, one earns this knowledge through lived research. And having learned, one can write, and in writing one learns more about what one claims to know. Before writers can give an audience an image of the world that is a creditable representation, they must sail the Seven Seas, or its equivalent.

No accidental tourist, learning for me often comes through incidental revelation, and these revelations inhere in artifacts, microscopic events with macroscopic implications. Let me offer some concrete examples and suggest what these examples have to do with writing and education.

Dissertations are sent to me from India in burlap wrappers stamped with wax seals at the seams. These wrappers usually have thirty or forty stamps because the average Indian doesn't buy stamps in larger denominations. The cost of sending a dissertation from North Bengal to Buffalo, even by "sea mail," is a king's ransom for someone who weaves hemp into rope: a month's salary at least. These packages bear many stamps of "registry," a holdover of the bureaucracy that the Raj imposed on the subcontinent.

These packages have a scent: an amalgam of mildew, sandalwood, and who knows what else – the smell of India. Countries, like bodies, have odors. When you receive, hold, smell, and read one of these dissertations with their courtly acknowledgments of "devoted mentors" and "sacrificial dons," you know that everything you write comes from a different place.

If you doubt it, I can let you smell a trove of Hong Kong scented matchboxes, which I keep as an olfactory heirloom on the shelf of my memorabilia highway. I went to Hong Kong and stayed for three years. I would not have gone, I think, had I not been sent a street map of Hong Kong by the HK Tourist Association at the request of the University of Hong Kong when I was considering responding to an ad for an academic post in the *New York Times*. Despite uncertainties and apprehensions about leaving home and all that that meant at that time of my life, I couldn't resist the splash of neon color in Victoria Harbor

– the glittering tracery of lights that run from Kennedy Town to North Point with the illuminated towers of Exchange Square and the Bank of China brightening the often sea-misty night sky.

I felt that I owed it to myself to test my inner wattage against the bright lights of this great Asian port. I came to understand that trade, commerce, the pegged Hong Kong dollar, the relentless flow of money and fluctuations of currency values and cross-rates drove those lights. One night I heard a Hong Kong trader ask a British investment banker, "What did you do today?" The Brit replied, "I watched money move." I came to see that F. Scott Fitzgerald's understanding of the relation of power to romance was accurate, but too tender in relation to the great realities of the world market.

I came to see that my American interest in introspection needed to be reexamined in the light of Hong Kong's obsession with interest rates. And when I flew from Beijing to Hong Kong and saw the contrast of South China's dim field of electric lights compared to the blaze above Hong Kong, I understood why so many mainland Chinese people were eager to be rejoined with Hong Kong.

I came to write about some of these things in fictional and nonfictional forms. One makes use of facts and artifacts in an effort to come to an imaginative understanding of another culture; and having the artifacts before one and in one's mind helps one remind oneself that difference is the key; that one needs to tame narcissistic self-indulgence, cultural arrogance, intellectual imperialism, absolutisms of all kinds.

Was I learning something important as I walked the streets of Central and looked always with pride at the LEGCO Building where the future of democracy in Hong Kong was being debated and fought for? Did the neo-classical pillars of that fairly modest structure, sitting in the center of Chater Square as an embodiment of the British Rule of Law, constitute a datum of relevant knowledge? There was nothing quite like it, finally, in Buffalo. I could see it only in Hong Kong.

My experience overseas, mostly in Asia Minor and Asia, leads me now as a teacher to pay attention to the cultural backgrounds of my students to the extent that I come to understand them. This is especially important at a time when major public universities serve diverse populations, including a large number of Asian-Americans. It is too easy in this environment to confuse, say, what I call traditional "Asian shyness" with passivity and a lack of imagination. It is equally easy to confuse a dedication to learning with submission to authority. Just the other day, an Asian-American student asked me, after I had read aloud Wordsworth's rather long "Tintern Abbey," if he would be required to memorize it for a quiz. And an exchange student from Korea sent her roommate to sit in on a class she had to miss so that the friend could take notes to help the foreign visitor improve her spoken English. I found this sense of responsibility touching and amusing, worthy of imitation by often-slack American students.

One needs to understand student behavior in terms of cultural difference, and one needs to understand that no two students are alike. Students come from different "worlds," whether that world is Bombay or Brooklyn, and every student is different from every other student and inhabits a unique world. If instructors use the lectern as a bully pulpit only for monologues, if they promote unchallenged abstractions, they should be encouraged to teach overseas for a while where they will learn quickly what it means to want to be understood on your own cultural and individual terms. Teachers who monopolize the space in a classroom should teach overseas and learn what it feels like to be marginalized.

To return to my beginning: The terrible conflict in Israel today, setting aside politics (if this is possible), is the result of a failure on all sides to accept the necessity for living with a respect for difference within the terms of a shared history. It is a dramatic and traumatic example of what can happen when a person or state attempts, with or without intention, to obliterate the identity of others who live in the same place at the same time. (We must find a way out of reciprocal annihilation as a form of politics.)

Albert Camus's "Appeal for a Civilian Truce" (1956) speaks to many levels of what I have been trying to say today with respect to education and culture:

> On this soil there are a million Frenchmen who have been here for a century, millions of Moslems, either Arabs or Berbers, who have been here for centuries, and several vigorous religious communities. Those men must live together at the crossroad where history put them.

We live at such crossroads every day, not least in our classrooms, where we have a chance, at a modest level, to apply the knowledge that we may have gained in our voyages out. And those voyages "out" will enrich the voyages "in" of writing and introspection. Travel-education-writing is a tripos: a three-legged stool upon which we usefully can sit as we look out our windows, home at last, pen in hand, computer humming, poised to re-create our world.

Re-vision

I imagined myself as a traveler in the greater world during the Second World War when it seemed to me that the world I wanted to live in might be destroyed. I first went to Europe in 1956-57 in search of art, culture, and romance; I returned with a deeper understanding of loneliness, my uncle's, and an increased awareness of the complexities of identity – individual and cultural. I went to Turkey in 1983-84 as an exile of sorts in the American provinces with a sense of mission – to help enlighten the world; I returned an internationalist and someone who had been enlightened about many aspects of life, especially the stabilizing role of tradition, if not repressive and enforced, in the life of the individual and family.

Each voyage out and each return tested a new set of assumptions about America and myself in relation to the larger world. I discovered that, in a sense, I belonged in no one place, even, perhaps especially, Israel where my daughter and her family live. My identity was layered in psychological, linguistic, aesthetic, and cultural terms. I belonged, to the extent that I belonged anywhere, in a symbolic world make up of the friends I had made along the journey with whom I felt a special affinity.

None of us belong wholly anywhere. A great deal of the conflict in the world stems from myths of belonging. This isn't to say that people don't need places and nations in which to live where they feel safe and in which they can live creative and productive lives. But it means that bitter, savage, and destructive conflicts might be avoided, at least ameliorated, if contesting groups could make room for the "other," recognizing that everyone is an "other" in some sense.

These essays compose something like a cultural autobiography, the subtitle of a talk I gave just before I left Hong Kong in 1994, of a man who came to understand his collective otherness, so to speak, a shared otherness. They are travel essays of a certain kind: a meeting place of self and world with each site of intersection serving as a tile in the mosaic of selfhood.

WORKS CITED

Bacon, Francis. "Of Travel." *The Essays of Lord Bacon.* Philadelphia: Henry Altemus.

Fitzgerald, F. Scott. "My Lost City." *The Crack-up.* ed. Edmund Wilson. New York:
New Directions Publishing, 1956.

Bate, William, and Frank Perry, eds. *Handbook for the Study of the United States.* Washington, D.C.: United States Information Agency, 1989.

Broder, David S. "The Loss of Two-Parent Families Damages Society," *IHT* (March 25, 1993).

Brogan, Hugh. *The Penguin History of the United States of America.* Harmondsworth: Penguin Books, 1985.

Eliot, T.S. "Tradition and the Individual Talent," *The Norton Anthology of American Literature.* Third Edition, Shorter. Nina Baym, *et al.*, eds. New York: W.W. Norton & Company, 1981.

Franklin, John Hope. *The Color Line: Legacy for the Twenty-First Century.* Columbia, MO: U of Missouri P, 1993.

Gilligan, Carol. *In a Different Voice: Psychological Theory and Women's Development.* Cambridge, MA: Harvard UP, 1982.

Harrington, Michael. *The Other America: Poverty in the United States.* Harmondsworth: Penguin Books, 1971.

Higham, John. "The New Colossus," Daniel J. Boorstin, ed. *An American Primer.* Chicago: New American Library, 1966.

Hoagland, Jim. "Endangered People Trouble the West's Environment," *IHT* (May 28, 1992).

James, Henry. "Hawthorne." *A Storied Land: Theories of American Literature.* ed. Richard Ruland. New York: E. P. Dutton & Co., Inc., 1976.

Lazarus, Emma. "The *Colossus,*" *A Nineteenth-Century American Reader.* Thomas M. Inge, ed. Washington, D.C.: United States Information Agency, 1987.

Pfaff, William. "Thus George Bush's America Passes Into History," *IHT* (November 9, 1992).

Pound, Ezra. "The Seafarer." *Ezra Pound Translations.* Intro. Hugh Kenner. New York: New Directions, 1963.

Slotkin, Richard. *Regeneration Through Violence: The Mythology of the American Frontier, 1600 1860.* Middleton, Conn.: Wesleyan UP, 1973.

Tavris, Carol, and Carole Wade. *The Longest War: Sex Differences in Perspective.* New York: Harcourt Brace Jovanovich, 1977.

Terms and Conditions of Grants for American Fulbright Grantees. Tokyo: The Japan United States Educational Commission, 1993.

Thoreau, Henry. *Walden and Civil Disobedience.* ed. Owen Thomas. New York: W. W. Norton & Company, Inc., 1966.

Turner, Frederick Jackson. *The Significance of the Frontier in American History.* Washington: Government Printing Office, 1894. Facs. Rpt. *March of America Facsimilies* Series 100. Ann Arbor: University Microfilms, 1966.

Young, Bonnie. *A Walk Through the Cloisters.* New York: The Viking Press, 1979.

Whitman, Walt. "Passage to India," *A Nineteenth-Century American Reader.* Thomas M. Inge, ed. Washington, D.C.: United States Information Agency, 1987.

Whyte, L. L. *The Unconscious Before Freud.* New York: Doubleday Anchor Book, 1962.

Wolf, Howard. *Broadway Serenade.* New Delhi: Academic Foundation, 1996.

Wolf, Howard. *The Education of a Teacher.* Buffalo: Prometheus Books, 1987.

ABOUT THE AUTHOR

Howard R. Wolf is Professor of English and Senior Fellow at The State University of New York (S.U.N.Y.) at Buffalo where he has been teaching since 1967. A graduate of Horace Mann School (NYC), Amherst College, Columbia University (MA), and The University of Michigan (Ph.D.), Dr. Wolf has been a Fulbright Lecturer in American Literature in Turkey (1983-84) and South Africa (1998). In spring 2007, he was a Senior Academic Visitor at Wolfson College, Cambridge University. Dr. Wolf is an essayist, short story writer, literary journalist, and autobiographer. During the past two decades, he has turned to what he calls "travel explorations." Published widely over the past forty years, he is currently working on a memoir about teaching and creativity and another book of travel letters. Howard Wolf's daughter and family live in Israel.